How to Create Chemistry with Anyone

How to Create Chemistry with Anyone

75 Ways to Spark It Fast . . . and Make It Last

Leil Lowndes

Vermilion
LONDON

1 3 5 7 9 10 8 6 4 2

Published in 2013 by Vermilion, an imprint of Ebury Publishing

First published in the USA in 2013 by Da Capo Press,
a member of the Perseus Books Group

Ebury Publishing is a Random House Group company

The Random House Group Limited Reg. No. 954009
Addresses for companies within the Random House Group can be found at
www.randomhouse.co.uk

A CIP catalogue record for this book is available from the British Library

The Random House Group Limited supports The Forest Stewardship Council (FSC®),
the leading international forest certification organisation. Our books carrying the FSC
label are printed on FSC® certified paper. FSC is the only forest certification scheme
endorsed by the leading environmental organisations, including Greenpeace. Our
paper procurement policy can be found at www.randomhouse.co.uk/environment

Printed and bound by CPI Group (UK) Ltd, Croydon, CR0 4YY

ISBN 9780091935450

Copies are available at special rates for bulk orders. Contact the sales development
team on 020 7840 8487 for more information.

To buy books by your favourite authors and register for offers, visit
www.randomhouse.co.uk

Contents

CHAPTER 3 _____

HOW TO SPARK CHEMISTRY TO ATTRACT   49

CHAPTER 7 _____

HOW TO SPARK CHEMISTRY FOR SEX   133

CHAPTER 8 _____

HOW TO SPARK CHEMISTRY FOR A RELATIONSHIP

Prologue

Love. The word is but a pale shadow of the ecstasy it brings us. We spend years, sometimes a lifetime longing for it. If we're lucky, we find it—and pray it lasts. But if it doesn't, we seek it again and again. Face it—we're hooked!

Cupid's quiver contains chemicals that bathe the brain and compel us to act in ways we can't fathom. When you have finished reading *How to Create Chemistry with Anyone*, though, you will. You'll know about love in a way that very few people currently do. And to the extent it is possible, you will be able to Spark romantic Chemistry with the man or woman of your choice.

You will also discover how and why nature injects you with different chemicals at various phases in your relationship and throughout your life. Finally, you will learn how to work with the changing Chemistry and create bonding chemicals so you both can "live happily ever after"—not just "until divorce do us part." Your new knowledge will not banish Cupid to the greeting card aisle, but it will help keep him in your life forever.

What Just Happened to Me?

You've felt it. Your heart pounds like a jackhammer, your tongue feels like sandpaper, your palms turn into a waterfall, and your words mysteriously start missing syllables. "Hello" becomes the hardest word in the English language.

But as your vital signs return to normal and a semblance of rationality sets in, you anxiously ask yourself if this person you just met felt the same Chemistry for you. If not, unrequited potential lovers used to think nothing could be done except sulk, swear, cry, or kick the cat. They were wrong, as you'll soon learn.

Why does this particular person blow you away like a tornado through a trailer camp, whereas with others, it's ennui at first sight? Because, unbeknownst to you, buried deeply in your brain, you have the ability to size someone up instantly.[1] This skill has strong evolutionary roots, dating from when an instantaneous "fight or flight" decision was a matter of life or death.

Throughout the centuries our crystal-ball capabilities have evolved with us. Just as DNA experts can tell a lot about a person from a sliver of his toenail, human beings have developed an incredible subconscious capability to sense whether someone will be fun to be with, fulfill their needs, and match a million other qualities on a very subjective laundry list of longings.

You've been setting the stage for love all through your life, just waiting for the star of the show to walk on the set. Your experiences from birth to the second you picked up this book draw a chart of the type of person you would—or even could—fall in love with. This map—your "LoveMap" as it is called—bears the mark of your unique individuality and can be specific down to details of physiognomy, personality, intellect, ambition, sense of humor, and hundreds of etceteras.[2] A very new field called "interpersonal neurobiology" also shows how your brain constantly rewires itself through your relationships.[3] Even a brief dalliance with someone you'd never want to see again could tweak your LoveMap forever.

By far the largest part of this map was charted in childhood before you were age five.[4] If you were fortunate, you were surrounded by people you loved and who loved you, primarily your relatives. Their proximity programmed a tendency in you to feel Chemistry with someone who looks like she could be from the same gene pool or the type of man who was around when you were a child. Have you ever noticed how many couples look alike?[5]

The influences on this diagram of who you could love ranges from milliseconds ago to millions of years before.[6] To complicate matters further, your memories get rewritten every time they are invoked. Is it any wonder that Chemistry is confusing?

How Fast Does Chemistry Happen?

How much time does it take to feel Chemistry? Compare the speed to a big ruckus in movie theaters back in the 1950s concerning subliminal advertising. Clever Madison Avenue types flashed words like "Hungry?" "Get popcorn!" and product names like "Lipton Tea" on the screen for less than a thousandth of a second during a movie. The messages flickered too fast for the audience to read. In fact, moviegoers reported they hadn't seen anything. But theaters sold a lot more popcorn on those particular days!

Unbeknownst to the audience, the "unseen" flashes on the screen not only made them hungry or thirsty; it also told them specifically what brands they wanted. Previously, moviegoers who used to order just tea now requested it by brand—Lipton, of course. Is it any surprise that neuroimaging shows you feel that Spark in a fifth of a second?[7]

Does Timing Count?

Unquestionably. It could have a lot to do with other events happening in life when you meet. Perhaps he is in love with someone else or maybe she just suffered a tragic loss. You might find yourself in conversation with a smart, sensitive, stunning, sensuous single someone who would be the perfect partner for you. This spectacular specimen of humanity blows you away instantly, but she is stifling a yawn. Or he is glancing over your shoulder for someone he'd rather talk to.

"What's wrong with me?" you scream at yourself between frantic heartbeats. Nothing. It's simply that thousands of other current emotional, physical, personal, or professional issues could close off his or her receptivity to you. Another time, another place, you might meet, and the magnetic field would make the two of you want to fall into each other's arms and bond together forever. Not only that, but for women it depends on the time of the month you meet![8] (More about that later.) Yes, timing counts.

What's Happening to My Brain?

Before you spotted this special person the one hundred billion nerve cells in your head were, relatively speaking, in what Cognitive Science calls "resting potential." But of course, they weren't really resting. The comparatively lethargic neurons were tediously *neurotransmitting* (we'll call it "texting") messages to each other about the weather, the boring party, the tasteless snacks, the whatever.

Then *KA-POW!* When your eyes spot this special someone across the crowded room, bar, bus station, McDonald's, or wherever, it's neurons gone wild! They hysterically contact their colleague neurons who live in other neighborhoods of the brain across tiny rivers called *synapses* to tell them the electrifying news. That's what neurologists call *action potential*—and what we call *Wow!*

Practically all of the techniques in the first sections of this book tell you how to create a neuronal response in someone to get feel-good chemicals, primarily one called *dopamine*. gushing into a brain region that Cognitive Science calls your *pleasure* or *reward center*. This response is so incredible that your target person gets a high, chemically similar to cocaine.[9]

Who Discovered Why We Feel Chemistry?

As you are reading this, neuroscientists are breaking new ground tracking the galaxy of nerve cells in your brain that are wired together with a million billion connections. Obviously, romance was not their motivation. These pioneering professionals' goal was far more significant, saving lives and preserving human physical and mental health. However, seekers of love benefit greatly by grasping their extraordinary contributions. We can now understand—and, to a certain extent, manipulate—the chemicals that marinate his brain or flow through her body when you meet. Let's call this person your "Quarry." And you are the "Hunter" or "Huntress" of hearts.

It is not only the cognitive community we must thank for unraveling the mysteries of romantic Chemistry; let's also tip our hats to evolutionary biologists and psychologists who further explore why we make such sudden and sometimes puzzling choices in relationships. These fields hold the key to why our neurons go berserk spotting one person and, comparatively speaking, hardly lift their sleepy heads for another.

But I Thought Chemistry Is Either There . . . Or It Isn't

Most people would agree with you. There are, of course, certain elements that, no matter what you say or do, can't change a thing when it comes to creating Chemistry. For instance, you can't change your or your potential partner's face, body, genotype, phenotype, or DNA. Additionally, by the time you are ready for love and sex, scillions of unconscious associations to pain or pleasure are etched in both your brains: How his stepdad dealt with him. How kindergarten schoolmates treated her. Who he previously loved. Who she hated. The instant you come into sight, all of the "whos," "whats," and "whys" of your potential partner's previous relationships resurrect neuronal activity from the past.

"Whew, if it's so complicated," you're thinking, "I can't possibly make my Quarry feel Chemistry for me." Sure, and people once thought, "The world is flat," "Heavier objects fall faster than light," and "All planets revolve around the earth." Scientists have tossed those three myths into the trash like dirty Kleenex. And the first just landed on top of them. Chemistry responds to very specific stimuli, many of which you *can* affect.

I do want to make one thing perfectly clear before we start, however: You can never have 100 percent control over a person's chemical reaction to you due to your Quarry's previous experiences, brain structure, and other factors listed above. But that's only part of the story. Mother Nature plays an equally large if not even bigger role in romance. You're going to learn how to be her coconspirator at the beginning of a relationship to capture your Quarry. Then you'll learn how to break away from the common forces that can demolish Chemistry between couples and destroy lasting love.

You are fortunate to be the first generation to benefit from fresh insights of Cognitive Science and the relatively new field called Developmental Evolution. Understanding what's in your Quarry's brain and how it develops will permit you to be more than just a pawn in nature's game. To a certain extent you can create specific chemically based emotions in the man or woman of your choice. The slight peek into neuroscience and new discoveries in evolutionary psychology in this book will give you further understanding of why and how you can create Chemistry and turn it into lasting love.

Chemistry Makes the World Go 'Round

They say "Love makes the world go 'round." But just as accurate is "Chemistry makes the world go 'round." Why? Because feeling Chemistry with someone is the precursor to passion, which leads to love, which leads to commitment. And that can lead to contentment, children, companionship, and many of life's greatest joys.

What do you think? Is feeling Chemistry and then falling in love a decision? A destiny? A choice? Some say you *decide* to fall in love. Sure, that's as easy as *deciding* to stop breathing or cherishing your children. Others say it's *destiny*. Well, move to an archipelago in Antarctica and wait for your *destined* one to come along. Many people think it's a *choice*. Of course, just like *choosing* not to eat, drink, or sleep.

Neurologists have proven that it is something else entirely. It is a *condition* that involves neurons, neurotransmitters, hormones, receptors, and circuits in your brain.[10] They define "being in love" as— get ready for a long sentence—an "elevated activity in the brain pathways which cause feelings of euphoria, strong motivation, and heightened energy which can induce sleeplessness, loss of appetite, and obsessive thinking about the beloved."[11]

That doesn't sound like much fun! And how crass to reduce it all to a rush of chemicals gushing through three pounds of gray slimy sponge under your scalp. Nobody wants to hear that, least of all me.

When humans first began to explore the sun, some people worried that God would be pushed aside. Likewise, some now fear discovering that love is simply a "condition" will make it less magic. Not at all! Understanding what love is just makes us a lot smarter in our choice of partner and teaches us how to keep that love alive.

Besides, who says a condition has to be crass or that a motivation system can't feel like magic? We know what it is. It's *love*, the greatest happiness known to humankind, and it has no parallel in human experience. Skeptics aside, love truly can last a lifetime and get better and better.[12] But only if you recognize the powerful neurological, chemical, and evolutionary forces controlling it.

Why Did It Happen?

Does it really matter? The two of you fell in love, and life will never be the same. You have found "the one"—the one you always knew would come along. Early love is the most exhilarating, extraordinary, ecstatic, and unforgettable part of the relationship. Your brain is brimming over with the intoxicating chemicals we'll soon meet called *dopamine, serotonin,* and incipient *oxytocin* and *vasopressin.* Hormones are at their highest levels ever. *Testosterone* and *estrogen* can hardly contain themselves. You and your lover want to cling tightly together and never part. "It's delightful, it's delicious, it's delectable, it's delirious," Mother Nature is urging. "Let yourself go!" This period is the best part—at least until the beauty of long-lasting lifetime love sets in.

So you cast off in the Love Boat with carefree abandon. But is it true that the course of true love never did run smooth? Sometimes it seems that way. Often, when embarking on a love affair, you think you are in control. When you first step into the Love Boat, it's like a sailboat on a calm sea on a sunny morning. Everything is beautiful. All's right with the world. You are sailing to Happily-Ever-After Land. An occasional gust of wind sweeps across the sea, and you break into song as it tingles your skin. Then the wind picks up, and that makes it even more exciting. You laugh out loud as you adjust the sails. The boat is a bit rocky, but you have faith it's propelling you toward ecstasy.

Suddenly the wind changes and you fear you may be going off course. What happened? What went wrong? The tempest makes you all the more desperate to get back on track. Your heart beats faster. But each time you think you've regained control, a bigger wind comes up.

Now there's an uncomfortable chill in the air, and the waves are rocky. Threatening clouds race across the sky and it starts to rain. The stabilizer cracks, and you desperately struggle to keep the boat afloat in the downpour. Soon darkness surrounds you, and you are helplessly tossed around. You are caught in the perfect storm. Will the Love Boat reach "happily ever after?" Or will it sink? It's up to you and how you'll use your new wisdom.

Are You the Master or the Slave of Love?

If only we could all be as wise in love as an Italian captain of a cruise ship, whom I'll introduce you to later, was in his profession. Captain

Giorgio Accornero was once offered the command of a 150,000-ton tanker. He refused. The flabbergasted shipowner asked, "But why? No captain has ever refused before. It is a great honor to be the master of such a large ship."

Captain Accornero replied, "Because, sir, I want to control the ship. I don't want her to control me."

The problem is that most people let the Love Boat master them rather than the other way around. The only way to be in control of the relationship is to admit that, in addition to magic, love is indeed a condition, a blissful one that we want to stay afloat forever.

Just as knowing how to create rain, feed animals, and nurture plants doesn't make the world less wondrous, likewise, wisdom about creating, feeding, and nurturing Chemistry doesn't make it less magnificent. In fact, knowledge about love gives you the ability to make love stronger and last longer.

Why Are We So Naive About Love?

Other than those life-sustaining needs like air, water, and shelter, I can think of no other need except love that begins at birth and lasts until we die. Yet I am shocked—no, stunned—by how little people know about this exquisite emotion that we idolize in music, film, and poetry, not to mention personally throughout our lives. We live for it. Some have died for it. In the song, "Oh Love," Brad Paisley and Carrie Underwood sang, "You're the simple truth. And you're the biggest mystery." Up until recently, that it was. Happily, however, love is no longer a mystery, and we're learning more about it every day.

For centuries philosophers, psychiatrists, and way too many lay people scratched their heads, made assumptions, and spouted theories about this phenomenon. Linguists, every bit as befuddled as the rest of them, wound up giving it a then-meaningless, cop-out name: "Chemistry." Little did they know how right they were!

Perhaps the wordsmiths were inspired by Aldous Huxley, who, in the early 1900s, wrote, "In one way or another, all our experiences are chemically conditioned."[13] In his day, thanks to visual tools like the telescope, scientists could explore outer space. But the astronomically closer inner space, the brain, was beyond the reach of the best of them. How ironic. They had the equipment to view planets light years away but not the tools to travel a few centimeters in the other direction. Today, however, extraordinary instruments like ƒMRI, CT, PET scanners, and a few other brain-imaging devices with mysterious acronyms permit cognitive neuroscientists to examine precisely what's going on in that wrinkly gray tofu between your ears.

The relatively new field of Cognitive Science—defined as the interdisciplinary study of the mind embracing philosophy, psychology, neuroscience, linguistics, and anthropology—is making phenomenal progress in putting pieces of the puzzle together. Although there are still unanswered questions—as there always will be in life—scientists have uncovered the influences that generate the electrochemical activity in your brain, making you feel that magical chemical Spark with someone. They have also discovered how identical chemicals can influence a male brain and a female brain and nervous system in very different ways.[14] Thus, the ways to Spark romantic Chemistry in this book will be gender specific—*very* gender specific!

Many people stubbornly insist that igniting Chemistry and making it last are not possible. They are wrong. Making it last is indeed doable, but *only* if you understand what kind of Chemistry we're talking about and work within the context of the following:

1. Your neuroanatomy is constructed in a very different way from that of the other sex, almost as different as your bodies.
2. Your brain is saturated by dissimilar drugs that dictate how you think, feel, and act as well as what you respond to.[15]
3. Distinct evolutionary influences are working on males and females.[16]
4. Mother Nature has carved out diverse roles for you.[17]
5. As a relationship matures, it is natural and unavoidable that different chemicals flood your brain and body, affecting your emotions and desires.[18]

I will give you techniques called *Chemistry Sparkers* to generate these specific bonding chemicals that keep you and your partner together. And, to the extent it is possible, regenerate some of the earlier thrilling ones.

Skull and Crossbones

Although love is the most exquisite emotion known to man and woman since the beginning of time, a sinister face sometimes hides behind an alluring mask. We all know beauty can be deceiving. If you're unaware of what you're dealing with, love can destroy you. Some people feel a Spark with someone who treats them badly because it's a familiar dynamic from childhood. Other common fragilities and shared unhealthy pathology can create damaging needs. Sadly, some people replicate these detrimental and sometimes risky relationships over and over again.

You've seen the TV ads for antidepressants that show previously despondent people dancing with delight through meadows tossing daisies at each other. Unless you listen carefully, you don't hear the lightning-speed voiceover saying, "Side effects may include nausea, vomiting, internal hemorrhaging, epileptic seizures, respiratory arrest, coma, loss of hair, impotency, and, in rare cases, death. Ask your doctor if [this medication] is right for you."

Likewise, when feeling that Spark, everyone is deaf to that internal voice warning, "Side effects may include hyperactivity, loss of appetite, trembling, obsessive thinking, compulsive acts, and symptoms associated with mental illness.[19] Ask yourself if [this particular person] is right for you."

Sometimes, when writing this book, I closed my laptop and gazed out the window, questioning whether I was writing a tutorial on how to create a bomb. The word *Chemistry,* in the sense we're using it, is indeed like a chemical weapon that, if you are not careful, can claim you as a victim. I hope you get more from this book than you thought you would. Like learning to tell which mushrooms are poisonous, I want you to realize when you should run from Chemistry with someone before it thrusts you into a rotten relationship.

Now the Good News

The other valuable lesson this book teaches is essential to your long-term happiness. Mother Nature makes the type of Chemistry between lovers change over time. Even in the best of relationships, it will. Don't let the books that tell you you'll want to jump each other's bones until you are eighty fool you. You can, however, create bonding chemicals that make love stay longer and generate delicious tides of sex more often. Unbeknownst to most people, these chemicals that replace the early hot ones are far more precious and essential to a fulfilling life than the sizzling kind. They are definitely not household names like *testosterone* and *estrogen*, and they are relatively unknown by people outside science-related fields; however, they are the essence of long-lasting happy relationships.

For the moment please use your new knowledge on how to create the more sizzling hot Chemistry that we'll talk about in the first sections wisely. Despite the overwhelming lust that you are absolutely sure is true love, slow down. Love can be as fragile and fleeting as an ice formation on the petal of a rose, or it can be as strong and enduring as an oak in the Petrified Forest.

Usually, if you are very young, it's more like the former. It has nothing to do with intelligence. You could be as smart as Albert Einstein, Steven Hawking, and Lisa Simpson all rolled into one, but no matter how brilliant you are, your neural connections are not fully developed until about age twenty-five.[20] In other words, you won't be able make the wisest decision about a partner until then. However, the love and passion chemicals gushing through your brain can blind you to reality at any age. That's part of Mother Nature's plan, which we'll discuss shortly. I pray this book will help you avoid the pattern of perceived love with the wrong person, marriage, disillusionment, divorce, and the tragedy of children left behind.

A Few Important Housekeeping Notes (Don't Skip These!)

Staring at the blank computer screen with my anxious fingers hovering above the keyboard, I had to make a few choices before tapping the first key. Here's what the Ouija Board decided.

Gender Grammar

Ah, the scourge of the English language, gender-specific pronouns! There was a day when the masculine "he," "his," and "him" graced most prose when referring to a nonspecific gender. Thankfully we are now an equal-opportunity pronoun language.

In the history of the world, however, there has never been progress without problems. The phrases "he or she" and "his or her" are unbearably clunky. Writer's Commandment Number One is "Thou shalt avoid clunkiness at all costs." So when a sentence is not gender specific, I will sometimes alternate "he" or "she" in the same paragraph. After much soul searching, I chose minor confusion over major clunkiness. I hope you won't find it too distracting.

You may also encounter the signs for male and female, ♂ and ♀ respectively. The techniques for Hunters are marked with ♂, and Huntresses with ♀. The Chemistry Sparkers for both sexes are indicated by ♀♂. You will find an almost equal number of Sparkers for men and for women. However don't skip the Sparkers for the other sex. Not only will they give you tremendous gender insights, but you'll also understand why your own Chemistry gets Sparked and by whom.

Gender Generalizations

Unfortunately, most sociological studies make a gross gender generalization saying females are primarily searching for a mate, and males just want a fling.[21] There are many millions of exceptions, but until proven otherwise, I'll follow their findings that this is primarily the case. Keep in mind, however, that most men do want to marry and settle down someday.[22] And I've yet to meet a modern woman who hasn't had a quickie tryst—or at least hasn't thought about it!

Developmental evolution shows that nothing is written in stone, especially human relationships. Are we headed toward a world of mainly Mr. Moms and predominately working wives? Probably not in our lifetime. But who knows what the future holds?

Same-Sex Relationships

Gay and lesbian Chemistry is every bit as powerful as opposite-sex relationships, and often their love can last even longer due to same-sex couples' neuroanatomical and neurochemical similarities. In this book, however, I speak primarily about male-female relationships because the structural, chemical, and functional brain differences are germane to the findings. They cause many of the most common relationship problems.[23]

Political Correctness

This brings me to a related maintenance issue. Should I obey or break the unspoken rule about avoiding gender stereotypes such as women being talkative and men being terse, women being in touch with their feelings and men asking, "What feelings?" I didn't have to think twice about this one because it is all biologically brain based. Whenever political correctness was contrary to the truth, I chose the latter.

Go ahead, PC police. Arrest me.

Places Where Singles Mingle

Happily, most meetings don't take place in a bar these days. Because many studies were conducted in pubs and at singles parties, however, I will sometimes use those locales as examples when speaking generically. Obviously, please dub in a venue more pertinent to your lifestyle, whether it's educational events, religious gatherings, concerts, or anywhere—including in front of your computer! The number of relationships that start with a cursor click is increasing exponentially. I'll also give you some deliciously devious but not untruthful ways to Spark Chemistry online before the first flesh-and-blood meeting.

Big Sparks and Little Sparks

There are two ways to Spark Chemistry. The most renowned is the instantaneous, split-second BLAM. Unfortunately, unless you fit in your Quarry's LoveMap—or invoke a "forgotten" intense adult experience—it's an almost-impossible task. So sometimes when I talk of "Sparkers," I'm referring to smaller pops that, when added up with a flurry of others, make the big Spark.

How to Make Anyone Fall in Love with You

Those of you who have read my first book on love by the above title will find this one quite different in two important ways. In *How to Make Anyone Fall in Love with You*, I shared eighty-five techniques to, as the title promised, make someone fall in love with you. Each "Little Trick," as I called them, was based on the latest sociological studies at the time. *How to Create Chemistry with Anyone*, however, deals with the most recent and current findings in the ground-breaking Cognitive Sciences and neuroimaging fields, which, when I wrote my previous book, were barely in their formative stages.

The best thing about my first book is that, as readers told me, the techniques worked. The worst thing is that some were a tad scheming. Although I never condoned lying, some methods involved presenting yourself in a way that magnified or minimized certain qualities depending on what your Quarry wanted. Now, with the new neuroscientific insights on love, however, retroactively I feel a bit guilty.

Mark Twain said that speaking with an uneasy conscience was like a having a hair in your mouth. Nowadays, when someone from the media asks me to tell their readers, listeners, or viewers some of the techniques from *How to Make Anyone Fall in Love with You,* I feel a follicle on my tongue.

So let's make a deal. I will give you techniques to kick your Quarry's nervous and hormonal systems into action. But when speaking with your Quarry, keep that hair out of your mouth! Don't misrepresent your qualities or magnify your attributes. Simply highlight the truths about yourself that relate to the pertinent Chemistry Sparking technique we're discussing. I say this not just on moral principles. When you embark on a serious love affair, any fabrication or falsehood could ruin two lives, your Quarry's and yours. Maybe more—your eventual kids'.

"Trailer" of What's Coming

Chapter 1, *Love in Limbic Land,* gives you a mini-tour of the territory (your Quarry's brain) and the tools (chemicals) you have to create Chemistry with him or her.

Chapter 2, *Chemistry at First Sight*, unravels the mysteries of that instant Spark that blows you away.

Chapter 3, *How to Spark Chemistry to Attract*, gives you twelve surprising techniques to ignite it. (Be prepared, some are extreme—but proven to work.)

Chapter 4, *How to Create Cyber Chemistry*, gives you six unique ways to Spark your Quarry into clicking on your dating site picture, then responding to your profile.

Chapter 5, *How to Spark Chemistry in Your First Conversation*, presents thirteen verbal Chemistry Sparkers to turn "Hello" into "Let's make a date."

Chapter 6, *How to Spark Chemistry on Dates,* furnishes thirteen techniques to keep things Sparking between you two every time you go out together.

Chapter 7, *How to Spark Chemistry for Sex,* provides ten unusual Sparkers to light erotic explosions in your Quarry's brain and keep them detonating time after time.

Chapter 8, *How to Spark Chemistry for a Relationship*, gives you eight techniques to turn a new relationship into a serious one—a seriously wonderful one.

Chapter 9, *How to Spark Chemistry for Falling in Love* provides five methods to make your Quarry want to take the tumble—into a beautiful life with you.

Chapter 10, *How to Spark Chemistry for a Lifetime of Love,* gives you eight methods to make beautiful beginnings last forever.

Sizzling Techniques Can Lead to Lasting Love

It is said that if you marry for any reason other than love, you pay for it every day for the rest of your life. Let me expand that. If you commit for the all-too-common initial madness of what you might mistake as "love," you also run that risk. Only if you marry with your new knowledge on what love is, and then nurture it, can "happily ever after" really happen.

The first half of this book gives you "little tricks" to Spark that initial erotic Chemistry. Some readers might call them "games." But ethical games have rules. The rules of this game of not-so-trivial pursuit are no deception, no dishonesty, and definitely no doing anything that would harm or mislead your Quarry. I warn you, however, that the ploys will involve a little strategy on your part—and also courage!

Women especially: you may be shocked to find the early flirtation techniques fripperous or outrageous. But absorb them because, as the content of the book deepens along with your relationship, you'll retroactively understand the wisdom behind them. You will learn how to turn sizzling sexy lure into significant long-lasting love.

Sources

Practically all the information in this book comes from original studies referenced in the back of the book. While proofreading the manuscript, however, I found that phrases like "a study proved," "the [name of journal] proved," and so forth were a snore. I fell asleep reading phrases like "the highly respected [neurologist, psychologist, sociologist, or anthropologist] found that . . . " So I decided simply to state the fact and put a reference number beside each. For more information on each subject, I invite you to visit the annotated original source in the back of the book.

There are hundreds of contributors to the neuroscience of love to whom I'm indebted, and you will find many of their names in the references. Let me take a second, however, to express my admiration and gratitude to three of them for their extra-special contributions to the material in this book. First to Dr. Helen Fisher, biological anthropologist at Rutgers who, in addition to original research, wrote several beautifully written books for the layman on the subject. I am also in awe of the fascinating studies by Arthur Aron, PhD (SUNY, Stony Brook,) and David Buss, PhD (University of Texas at Austin) concerning the cognitive and evolutionary aspects of relationships. And a personal note of gratitude to my friend and "fact checker," Dr. William Hoffman. This esteemed neurosurgeon made sure I followed the convoluted paths of the human brain accurately and didn't drown in some of its synapses.

A multitude of research substantiates each fact in this book. For conciseness, however, I cite only one or two landmark studies on each finding. In my previous book, *How to Make Anyone Fall in Love with You*, I also referenced a great many studies. Except when absolutely necessary, I avoided citing those again.

The Only Fiction You'll Find

Anyone who has witnessed the blue of the sky on a clear day, the green of the grass in spring, and the brightness of the sun at midday realizes Mother Nature's breathless beauty. Anyone who has survived a tornado, a blinding snowstorm, or a tempest at sea is in awe of her power. And anyone who has fallen in love has unknowingly been her ecstatically willing pawn—for better or for worse. Mother Nature's main task is to keep the earth flourishing by assuring that all fish in the sea, birds in the sky, plants of the land, and mammals on earth, including humans, go forth and multiply.

The personification of this powerful force is the only fiction. Other than that, the entire book consists of information (proven), stories (true), and humor (weak).

How Complicated Is It?

Some of you have already surmised that, considering the magnitude of the subject, *How to Create Chemistry* is, to say the least, simplified. I do this because the riveting field of Cognitive Science, which covers so many disciplines, needs a little simplification!

To readers who are more knowledgeable about Cognitive Science, I beg your pardon in advance for the oversimplification. *How to Create Chemistry with Anyone* is written in layman's language. Sometimes too layman. Enjoy!

CHAPTER 1

Love in Limbic Land

Where do we feel love? If you asked most people, they would answer, "In the heart, of course." Valentine's Day proves it, right? Lovers give and receive cards, pendants, and chocolates in the shape of hearts. We carve our names surrounded by a heart in tree trunks and tell each other, "My heart belongs to you." Only a fanatic neuroscientist would insist on accuracy. He would send his ladylove a Valentine's Day card with the image of a squishy gray blob evocative of a rotting cauliflower, the brain, because that's where romance really resides.

Where Love Lives

Love dwells where all your emotions do, in the region I'm calling "Limbic Land." More correctly, Cognitive Science labels it your *limbic system*. It's the part of your brain that houses the laughs, the tears, the hopes, the disappointments, the anger, the ardor, the ups, the downs, the in-betweens, and the profounds. The seed of *all* your emotions resides in your limbic system, and one of the most powerful is love. Someday it will be a household word. Instead of saying, "Don't get so emotional about it," chastising family, friends, and lovers will say, "Oh, don't get so limbic!"

Let me present the five main residents of Limbic Land in alphabetical order. The "relationship chemicals," which I'll introduce afterward, affect regions of a ♂ brain and ♀ brain differently. Limbic Land is a very sexist place to live.

Your Amygdala Nickname: Ms. Emotions

I hesitate to present this brain region first because the *amygdala* is hands down the emotional leader of Limbic Land. In love she can sometimes be flaky and totally irrational. But after you've read this book you'll never again need to tear your hair out over your partner and scream, "She's nuts!" or "He's an animal!" You will understand *why* the two sexes are so different.

It should come as no surprise that women have a larger, deeper limbic system than men do.[1] But here's some happy news for Huntresses: A man's love is often stronger and can last even longer for reasons to be explained.[2]

A Huntress also has a more direct neurological connection to her *amygdala* because her neurons are more tightly packed.[3] In fact, they have an ongoing dialogue about her day-by-day, night-by-night relationship with her Quarry. Think of the female brain's neurons as a group of women walking along on a clear day in the bright sunshine, all talking to each other at the same time. They are so close to each other that, amazingly enough, they don't miss a word.

Conversely, a male thinks primarily with his gray matter, of which he has six and a half times more of than a female.[4] Gray matter is very good stuff because of its great ability to focus.[5] Picking up on subtleties or communicating emotions, however, is not gray matter's specialty.[6]

Imagine a Hunter's grey matter neurons are like a scattered herd of guys plodding along a rocky path in the pouring rain and gusty wind. They're so far apart that they'd have shout to even hear each other, let alone make any sense out of what the other guys are saying. Is it any wonder that women are more in touch with their emotions?

Your Hippocampus Nickname: Mr. Memory

The *hippocampus* is memory—short term, long term, and, most of the time, subconscious. This other Limbic Land dweller also has a closer relationship with the *amygdala* when it comes to emotional issues in the female brain. It drives a Hunter crazy when his wife or girlfriend remembers all the details of the inconsiderate thing he did, the insinuation he made, or the birthday he forgot. "Why can't she just let it go?" he agonizes. Sorry, guys, it's not her fault. The more closely knit team of her *hippocampus* and *amygdala* won't let her.

Your Hypothalamus Nickname: Mr. Action

Now comes the part everyone in the brain wants to influence, your *hypothalamus,* which shoots messages down the spine 24/7, controlling your central nervous system. He's the strong man who makes you physically act and react. Blame this brain region when, upon feeling that Spark of Chemistry, your mouth goes dry, your heart skips a beat, and your flushed face resembles a radish.

Your *hypothalamus* deals with sex, big time, especially in guys. In fact, it's more than twice as large in the male brain, and has an excellent working relationship with *testosterone.*[7] This brain region is in charge of the temporary growth of a significant male append-age at tender moments—and *testosterone* cheers him on. In addi-tion to erections, the *hypothalamus* also monitors entities (at certain times considered secondary by men) such as eating, sleeping, and breathing.

Your Caudate Nucleus and Environs
Nickname: Pleasure Island

Before we get to the "brainy" part of your brain, let's get to the hap-piest. It's a region called your *caudate nucleus*. This feel-good area encompasses the *nucleus accumbens* and the nearby *ventral tegmen-tal area (VTA)*. Combined, Cognitive Science calls it your *pleasure* or *reward center*. Excitement, enjoyment, and exhilaration hang out there. After a few gulps of a certain love chemical that I'll introduce next, *Pleasure Island* lights up like a Las Vegas slot machine. Life would be hardly worth living if it weren't for this happy neighbor-hood in your brain.

Your Prefrontal Cortex Nickname: The Professor

Last but most assuredly not least is the wisest part of your brain, which we're nicknaming the *Professor*. The *prefrontal cortex* does not live in la-la *Limbic Land* with the rest of the cast *of Chemistry*. His throne is at the front of your brain. This sage assiduously reviews neurotransmissions (which we'll call "texts" or "tweets") from *Limbic Land* and tries to determine who is bad for you, who is better for you, and who is best for you.

Unfortunately, most new lovers don't listen to the *Professor*. When a couple is in the early hot love "condition," Mother Nature is blasting their brains with so many intoxicating chemicals that the signals from the rational brain section are weaker.[8] The *Professor* tries to prevent lovers from making a fool of themselves and doing self-destructive things while smitten. But when in love, who listens?

That's the emotional housing complex of the brain. Bear with me while I now introduce the chemicals that live inside. They play the biggest roles in love, and knowing about them is necessary to understand how to create Chemistry with someone.

The Six Sexy Chemicals of Love

Dopamine

The star of the early show in love is *dopamine*. He's on the scene every time you feel sudden Chemistry with someone, and his influence is mind-blowing. (He has helper chemicals like *norepinephrine* and *phenylethylamine*, but he's the leader when you're "crazy in love.") When you first meet *dopamine*, he introduces himself as ecstasy, euphoria, exaltation, exhilaration, and intoxication. Sometimes he appears in a split second; at other times he creeps up slowly. As you're falling in love, he scoops you up and whisks you off to that most beautiful place you will ever go, *Pleasure Island,* or the *caudate nucleus,* located deep in your limbic system.

Dopamine loves action and jumps into the fray when you feel fear. That's why movie thrillers filled with bloody bodies and crashing cars give some people a kick. *Dopamine* is also summoned by beautiful music, stirring sermons, and activities you enjoy. People do desperate things to make him stay because, if he disappears or starts slipping away, they can become despondent, even self-destructive.

In fact, he has such a powerful ecstasy influence that many of today's most credible anthropologists, neurologists, and psychiatrists say that love is simply *dopamine*'s effect on the *pleasure center* in your brain.[9] Personally, I don't like to think of it that way, but the evidence makes a pretty good case.

Did someone liken this chemical to cocaine? Yes, everybody with even a passing knowledge of Cognitive Science does.

Serotonin

When *serotonin* is high in your system, you feel superb. This blissful chemical floods your brain when you exercise, genuinely laugh, sunbathe, go sailing, skiing, surfing, dancing, or do anything else you love. She is so central to your happiness that if she starts to shrink drastically, you become melancholy, morose, and miserable. Some sad souls turn to alcohol—or worse—just to bring her back for short visits.

Ideally, *serotonin* and *dopamine* would work well together. But there is a problem. If *dopamine* makes you act too frenetic about your relationship, *serotonin* doesn't like that. She'll start shrinking away, leaving you with insomnia, eating disorders, negative thoughts, anxiety, and worse. When *serotonin* is artificially introduced, such as in antidepressants, she can also mess with your ability to love.[10] It's up to couples to keep *serotonin* and *dopamine* in balance working together, without medication.

Testosterone

Need I even introduce this famous performer? It is the most revered and reviled romance chemical of all. Sometimes *testosterone* gets a bad rap and people blame him for starting street brawls, civil wars, stabbing adversaries in the back, piloting corporate takeovers, driving too fast, robbing, raping, sleeping around, and channel surfing. Although some of these unsavory types are, indeed, high-T men, it's not all true. *Testosterone* is a good guy who plays a big role in developing creativity, intellect, thought patterns, assertiveness, and drive.[11] He also gives guys large muscles, increased bone mass, and, of course, colossal, sometimes uncontrollable, sexual desire.

Estrogen

Equally well known, *estrogen* is a hot commodity for women. Those who want to look younger and more beautiful—like 100 percent of the world's female population—crave her effects. Lucky ladies blessed with a lot of this hungered-after hormone have clearer complexions, shinier hair, rosier cheeks, fuller lips, larger breasts, and they are generally healthier. High-*estrogen* women also get pregnant more easily. Due to Mother Nature's influence, that is a (very) subconscious Chemistry Sparker for guys, as you will soon learn.

This leads us to the family-friendly chemicals.

Oxytocin

Oxytocin is wonderful. Everybody loves her because she generates affectionate feelings, increases trust, and promotes long-lasting relationships. It would be an exaggeration to say that *oxytocin* is more of a woman thing, and the next "togetherness chemical," called *vasopressin*, a guy thing. Male and female brains create both. However, mixed with *estrogen*, *oxytocin* has a powerful bonding effect.

Oxytocin and her colleague chemical, *vasopressin*, help keep lovers together and make them more devoted parents.[12] Neurologists don't call them the "bonding" or "cuddle chemicals" for nothing, and we'll learn more about them later in the book.

Vasopressin

Vasopressin's effects are similar to *oxytocin*'s, and the two often have the hyphenated name *oxytocin-vasopressin*. They are both family folks. The latter does a terrific job of making a man bond with his lifetime partner and become a more involved dad.[13] Unfortunately, *vasopressin* and *testosterone* don't get along well together. The former can drive the latter down.[14] Because he's not coming on to his wife as much after childbirth, a wife often mistakenly fears the new dad is not sexually attracted to her anymore.[15] But, women, look on the bright side: It means he's bonding better with you and the baby. Besides, less *testosterone* reduces his desire to seek sex elsewhere.

Girl, I know what you're thinking, but don't hold your breath. It will be a while before some profit-hungry drug company gets FDA approval for a *vasopressin* pill you can slip in your man's orange juice.

Now, let's talk about your specific qualities, which will play a major role in Sparking your Quarry's Chemistry, and how to get Mother Nature to help you do the job. You may wonder why I'm breaking it down into body parts. It's because the information is crucial to the Sparking techniques.

CHAPTER *2*

Chemistry at First Sight

As you read in the Introduction, due to DNA, past experiences, and a myriad of other elements, you can never have 100 percent control over the Chemistry between you and someone. That's just part of the picture, though. Mother Nature plays a *huge* role. In fact, she is your best friend in helping you Spark your Quarry. Animals follow Mother Nature's guidance instinctively. When another of their species excites them, they growl, grunt, cluck, crow, pant, or emit some other form of indigenous whooping it up. (Humans have to be a bit more subtle about it.)

Animals strive to entice the best mate according to the neurological, chemical, and evolutionary influences defining "best" in their species. Although you may not think of it that way, but you do too. Something else comes into the human equation, though. You have a bigger brain and are, unfortunately, restricted by certain social conventions. Because you are more complicated, the Sparking process is too.

"All Men Are Animals"

Huntresses, have you or a friend ever complained, "Guys are only interested in sex"? If not, you've probably thought it. My girlfriend Brandy from Boston certainly does. Brandy is a beautiful woman, a serial dater, and a constant complainer about men. She comes to New York every year to run the marathon. Here is our annual ritual: The night before the big event, we go to the same restaurant for the same pasta with olive sauce, and I listen to her same gripes about the men in her life.

Last November, twirling spaghetti around her fork and making direct eye contact with a pimento-stuffed olive, she griped, "Guys are only interested in sex. They're all big penises with a man attached. From the first date, they're pressuring me. Why can't I find a man I can connect with? Someone I can talk to . . . a guy who talks to me, not my breasts? I want a guy to cuddle, not fall asleep right after sex. Is that too much to ask?"

"Well, Brandy, that last part is." I started to tell her about the universal male condition called "postcoital narcolepsy" and the chemical reason a man can't help zonking out after ejaculation.[1] But she cut me off. There is no stopping Brandy once she's on a roll.

In previous Novembers I just nodded while she went on and on. But this year, while writing *How to Create Chemistry*, I could hold it in no longer. I interrupted her diatribe and said, "Well, hell-OH, Brandy, what do you expect?"

Shocked, she glared at me. "What . . . what do you mean?"

"Brandy, my dear friend, you can take a male out of the jungle, but you can't take the jungle completely out of the male. In fact you wouldn't want to. Usually a guy's initial motive for even asking you out is because he wants sex, the sooner the better. He doesn't want to spend all night touching your soul. He'd prefer to touch your breasts. Brandy, you have to give it time!"

"Sure," she said rolling her eyes. I would have continued, but I knew she needed sleep to face the challenge she'd been training for all year. I hugged her and gave her my annual "Tear up the road tomorrow, Tiger." Then I made a mental note to send her this book.

So was Brandy wrong about men? Sex is definitely not the only thing most men think about when asking you out—just usually the first.[2] In addition to some of the aforementioned elements, it is what makes a guy feel that Spark for a particular woman. Most men do want a permanent relationship eventually.[3] But sexual attraction is crucial because it's the match that lights the fire. Deep conversations, communicating, connecting, and commitment come later.

"All Women Are Gold Diggers"

If you've read my previous books, you are familiar with Phil, my dear friend and platonic male housemate, or "friend without benefits." Phil makes my personal research into the male psyche quite convenient. Besides, he's the best housemate a gal could ever have. Naturally, every time he comes home from a date, I grill him mercilessly about it.

One night Phil returned with that "She was the date from hell" expression on his face. His wobbly walk and martini breath told me he'd consumed more than his customary one drink. He obviously wasn't in the mood to submit his social report.

As I was attempting an "I'm not the least bit curious" expression, my mild-mannered roomie uncharacteristically grumbled under his breath, "Freakin' gold digger!" The usually fastidious Phil tossed his coat on the couch and staggered unsteadily toward the bathroom. Under the rumble of his electric toothbrush, I heard him bellowing something in French, which he doesn't speak. "Le Bernardin, Le Bernardin, Le Bernardin!"

"Did you say something, Phil?" I called.

He opened the door and, Crest foaming out of the sides of his mouth, shouted, "Le Bernardin! It's the most %@!& expensive restaurant in New York!" Spitting out the foamy water, he continued, "This afternoon, I texted her the name of the restaurant where I wanted her to meet me. But oh no, that wasn't good enough for Goldilocks! She texted back that she preferred a 'nice little restaurant' near where she worked. Oh, it was nice all right. The bill came to over two hundred dollars, and all evening she's asking me creepy questions. Oh, ho ho. I read between the lines with no problem. She was trying to figure out how much money I make. Damn gold digger!" he bellowed as he slammed his bedroom door.

Of course, money is not a woman's major criterion for a man. However, no matter how much she herself has, Mother Nature is whispering in her ear, "Make sure he'll be a good provider for you and your eventual babies, dear." Even if she earns enough herself to put an entire orphanage through college, most women feel her man should earn more than she does.[4]

Huntresses, Cut the Animals Some Slack

Sisters, his constant pressure for sex is not his fault. You wouldn't blame a guy for limping due to a birth defect. Likewise, you can't blame him for his greater sexual drive, which nature also programmed into him before he was born.[5] It's an almost insurmountable challenge for a male to push sex out of his mind. Mother Nature (MN for short) injected men at least with ten times more testosterone than you. It's not an exact proportion, but think about it: If you were ten times more ravenous for sex, wouldn't you act a little more needy, greedy, and aggressive about it? Women can go for months, sometimes years, between relationships without sex. But for men, it's practically impossible.[6]

In fact, a guy's testosterone level shoots up a full third even casually chatting with a female stranger![7] Just thinking of you being naked makes dopamine gush through his brain like a cocaine rush. Unfortunately, that feel-good chemical short-circuits messages en route to his prefrontal cortex, the thinking part of his brain. Consider the ever-lengthening list of male politicians, sports figures, and other celebrities who throw away valuable careers for a few rolls in the hay. Girl, you have the power to turn a dignified gentleman into a dyslexic octopus when he's around you.

Sex Scrambles His Brain

In fact, guys don't just make dumb decisions about sex; they can make pretty dangerous ones. Researchers on the Florida State University campus gathered a group of gutsy girls and directed them to approach male students they didn't know and ask, "Will you have sex with me tonight?" Seventy-five percent of the guys agreed immediately.[8] That shocked even the relatively unshockable me. More recently, in a follow-up study after AIDS awareness, 69 percent of the males agreed.[9] That stunned me even more and made me very, very sad.

Needless to say, when the study, "Gender Receptivity to Sexual Offers," was reversed, and men approached the female students, none of them agreed to sex, pre- or post-STD awareness.

Blame Mom and Co.

Here is yet another complication. The guy brain is spinning with mixed signals. He probably grew up with a mother who implied that anything sexual was naughty. Maybe she scolded him for looking at his sister when she was dressing. Or was furious when she caught him looking at "nasty pictures" in magazines. She told him to keep his hands off his tiny crotch in public. One of my seminar students told me that his mom once spanked him when she walked into his room and caught him masturbating. In short, little guys grew up thinking sex was dirty.

Then suddenly, a whole new set of signals replaced it. His high school buddies bragged about their sexual conquests; many self-proclaimed studs exaggerate them to gain status in their friends' eyes. No guy wants to admit he's still a virgin, so he becomes obsessed with curing himself of that "contemptible" condition. The social pressure to score is tremendous.

I learned that at my girlfriend Sheila's sixteenth birthday party. At one point while we were talking, she leaned toward me and whispered, "What are those boys doing over there?" Five or six of them were comparing something they'd taken out of their pockets.

"I think it's their combs," I guessed.

"They must be pretty old," she murmured, "because it looks like some of them lost a lot of teeth." When one boy proudly held up a totally toothless comb, they all cheered. Sheila called across the room, "Hey, guys, whatcha doing?" That detonated an outburst of hilarity that would have merited the acronym ROTFL. They were literally rolling on the floor laughing.

It wasn't until a week later that Sheila and I managed to wrestle her brother to the floor and demand he tell us what was going on at the party. Gasping for breath, he was forced to rat on his buddies. "The guys were comparing combs. Every missing tooth represented sex with a different girl."

A male who sleeps around is enviably called a "stud." A female with the same sleeping habits is disparagingly called a "slut." Fair? No. Understandable? Yes, at least in terms of evolutionary psychology.

Hunters, Cut the Gold Diggers Some Slack

It is impossible for a female to close her ears to the cries of her ancient foremothers. Here is her recurring subconscious nightmare: After a stupendous night of sex with you, you hop onto your trusty steed and ride off into the sunset . . . alone. She is left pregnant. Your fifteen minutes or so of bliss could mean fifteen years or so of burden for her.

"But that's not going to happen," you protest. Of course it isn't. She knows that too. But speak to the sticky cognitive modules floating around in her brain. Consult with her Cro-Magnon grandmother. Subconsciously she does, and the response is always, "It happened to me, dearie, it can happen to you." Her primeval grannies also remind her that she will suffer morning sickness, migraines, throwing up, leg cramps, and hip pains.

Gentlemen, a bad bout of morning sickness is the same sensation you'd feel after scarfing down seafood cocktail and a dozen raw eggs, followed by a Big Mac, a hot fudge sundae, and a six-pack of beer. And then deciding to go for a spin on the roller coaster.

If your girlfriend gets pregnant, she pays a big biological cost. You can't have another whole human being residing inside you without crowding your own body space and causing some huge hassles, like sharing calcium, iron, vitamins, and other elements crucial to health and beauty.

Then there's the weight gain, the dumpy clothes, and no sex. If you don't believe it, put a cement block inside a beach ball and strap it to your stomach. Then try to have sex.

After that is the excruciating pain of childbirth, followed by changing diapers, the terrible twos, the tantrum threes, the fiendish fours, the feisty fives, and so on. Because her plight won't permit her to work through the early childrearing process, can you see why your financial status is at least a factor? Primordial memories stick like glue, so is it any wonder that a woman doesn't want to jump into bed with you right away?

Your biological cost as a male? Zip. You only spin off sperm to start the whole process, and that's a whole lot of fun. Gentlemen, I applaud you. It is truly charming, if not naive, that when you fall deeply in love, you become blind to some of the realities of life.[10] Females are usually more sensible about partner choice. Brain-imaging studies of women in love show activity in many more areas than yours.[11] However, when a guy has flipped, in a sense, he's *really* flipped, because more of his critical thinking pathways close down.[12] She's making her decision with more of her head, whereas yours are made with, well, more of your other body parts.

Be thankful that most women are more realistic in relationships. If she were as resistant to the reality of resources as you are when you fall in love, there would be more miserable marriages of the all-too-common kind in which he is broke, she's freaking, and the kids are hungry. Bottom line, brothers: Respect your Quarry's realization, that, in the long run, you really can't live on love alone.

Here's food for thought: Is her immediate consideration of your wealth any worse than you immediately considering how physically attractive she is—and how soon she'll go to bed with you?

What Sparks a Hunter's Chemistry—and Why?

Huntresses, if any of you are still harboring any doubt that your looks are the first thing a man cares about, let me quote one landmark study that doesn't mince words: "A woman's physical attractiveness is the cardinal component of women's mate value."[13] "Mate value" is the crass word that researchers use for how desirable someone is in the "meat market." Yep, Huntresses, your looks matter, big time, at least until he gets to know you and your amazing qualities.

A man can be sexually turned on by a gorgeous woman he would never dream of having a relationship with—a mindless model, a knockout with bust size 38 and IQ to match, or a hot lady of the night he would be ashamed of the next morning. Those lasses may be delicious company for one night, maybe two if they're lucky. But definitely not someone he'd want to raise a family with. When thinking of a date, many guys' fantasies of the future end at orgasm.

The specifics may seem obvious. However, in this section I want to quickly review the particulars of what excites males, because only when you understand *why* your Quarry gets whacked over certain features can you confidently and courageously use the Chemistry Sparkers in the next section.

Babies "R" Us

Guys don't realize it themselves and would surely deny it, but the number one subconscious Chemistry Sparker boils down to one word: *fertility*. Procreation is the name of nature's game. It's the bottom line, the nitty gritty of what guys find hot.[14] Science calls it like it is: "Instinctively, the male of all species wants to get the 'biggest reproductive payoff' for his," ahem, "investment."[15] After all, Mother Nature figures, why should a guy squander his sperm in a woman who can't bear him a healthy baby with good genes and a strong immune system? That would be a humongous waste of time.

Gentlemen, even if you are planning a peaceful life without the smell of baby poop and getting barfed on, Mother Nature doesn't know that. She programs you to be attracted to a female who looks like she'd be a good baby factory.

Sisters, Big Mama's got it all rigged to help that along. At ovulating time she gives you a natural cosmetic makeover and even makes you more symmetrical.[16] Your eyes get larger, your lips get fuller, and your cheeks become rosier during the big O days (ovulation, not orgasm).[17] It's like female apes whose lower cheeks get redder when they're in estrus. In case any guy ape would miss it, she grows a humongous pink butt at target time. Similarly, your rosy facial cheeks subconsciously signal guys that it's the best time to "make the shot."

Incidentally, ladies, if the big tough High-T guys aren't usually your preference, be extra vigilant during those big "O" days. MN slips you a chemical cocktail that makes you more attracted to them when you're most apt get pregnant.[18]

Let's Break It Down to Body Parts. Guys Do.

A Hunter doesn't look at you and specifically think, "Wow, smooth skin, big breasts, narrow waist, long shiny hair, and youth." It's the whole package that hits his eyes. But to have more "ammunition" on your hunting expedition, I'll tell you why each element counts.

Smooth Skin. Skin is a measuring stick for your hormonal state, which is, incidentally, more detectable in the lighter skin of blondes.[19]

That's why it is said that "gentlemen prefer blondes." Do you remember the classic Marilyn Monroe film by that name? If a biologist were naming the film, it would have a less catchy but more telling title like, "Gentlemen prefer females with lighter hair and skin to more easily detect anemia, cyanosis, jaundice, and other skin diseases."[20] But then the movie wouldn't have been a box-office blockbuster.

Long Hair. Even short, shiny hair signals health and estrogen and, thus, that you're more easily impregnable. But long, shiny hair shows you've been healthy and chock-full of that enviable hormone for a couple of years. Natch', that means you'd be easier to impregnate with a healthy baby.[21]

While we're discussing hair, here's a bit of trivia that has absolutely no scientific basis, simply something from a men's website survey. Rather than the bushy look downstairs, the majority of men prefer the more youthful, completely shaved or famous "landing strip" look of Brazilian fame, shaved on both sides evenly.

I once told my hairdresser that I had a great business idea for her: She should open a chic pubic hair trimming salon. I've had a lot of bad business ideas.

Hourglass Figure. So what's the big deal about a shapely body, you ask? Mother Nature murmurs in his ear, "Dude, she'll get pregnant faster and easier and is less apt to have a miscarriage.[22] A male subliminally recognizes that Ms. Shapely's roomier hips would give his unborn progeny's head more room to expand. To add more fuel to his firing neurons, her bigger breasts signal about 37 percent more estrogen.

Eyes? Larger "ovulating signaling" eyes are a bigger draw. Concerning color, blue-eyed men are drawn to similarly light-eyed women because it's a good cuckoldry indicator that his little one didn't have a brown-eyed daddy.[23]

Hey, What About My Face? I always thought a woman's face was the first thing a Hunter looked at, so I was shocked at the studies that report a male registers your body first.[24] He probably doesn't even realize it himself, but nanoseconds beforehand he has subconsciously sensed your body to see if your face is "worth checking out." Disbelieving, I decided to ask Giorgio, the ship's captain I mentioned earlier who subsequently became my guy. Giorgio is an extremely cultured gentleman, so I naturally assumed that he'd say "her face."

"Giorgio, if you could choose between a woman with an averagely attractive body and a spectacular face, or a dynamite body and an average face, which would you choose?" I couldn't have counted to one before his answer zapped back, "The latter." I sucked in my stomach and slunk back to the studies.

A few weeks later, while rearranging my library, I came upon my freshman yearbook. Flipping through it reminded me of something that happened the first night in my new dorm that should have given me a clue way back then. A senior was showing us the previous year's book and chatting about some of the girls we'd soon meet on campus.

"And here's Shelly," she said pointing to one headshot. Several of us had to stifle an insensitive smile. It is only a slight exaggeration to say her face could have been the prototype for the Muppet's Miss Piggy. Our senior informant went on, "The guys are crazy about her." The rest of us looked at each other in shock.

A few weeks later I met Shelly at the campus pool. Her face was, indeed, evocative of the Muppet celebrity, but certainly not her body. She had the breasts of Beyoncé, the butt of Jennifer Lopez, and the waist of a wasp. And to think I still wondered why guys were so attracted to her.

Does My Age Matter That Much? Despicable perverts aside, a young girl doesn't usually begin Sparking a Hunter's Chemistry until she begins to get curvy around the time her periods start. Even preteen guys fantasize about older girls when they're all alone in their bedrooms with their doors locked.[25] Mother Nature figures, "Why fritter away fantasies on girls who can't get pregnant?"

This brings us to an unsettling but inevitable fact: We grow old. So do guys, but that's no problem for Big Mama in the sky. She figures men can still spread sperm in younger women for as long as they can get it up. Depressingly, after menopause Mother Nature makes a female's breasts and butt start to sag, nipples soften, waists thicken, lips thin, complexions roughen, cheeks pale, and hair lose its shine. Personally, I think MN gave us a raw deal. She's telling guys, in no uncertain terms, "That old lady is no longer fertile. So screw her—or, rather, don't."

What Sparks a Huntress's Chemistry—and Why?

Hunters, whenever a clearly stunning female slinks into the room, male eyeballs start to whirl like a beanie cap. So you probably assume that a great-looking guy—tall, big muscles, flat abs—would spin females' heads. In another era you would have been right. A cave woman needed a mate with enormous muscles to bash a wild boar on the head and spacious shoulders to carry the bloody beast home. Tall was better too, because he could run faster if he missed his target. The cave lady wanted her man oozing testosterone out of every pore, signifying aggression, high sexual desire, and strong genes to bear beefier babies.

In those days selecting a sensitive, compassionate, loving male would have been a really lamebrain choice. Imagine a caveman's success at intellectually reasoning with the tiger poised to pounce on him. If the ferocious animal didn't concede, her little one would have no daddy. So Mother Nature poked the primitive pretty and said, "Better to go with the powerful jerk, dear."

Being drawn to brawny guys with a touch of the brute lasted a surprisingly long time. A scant fifty years ago women swarmed to movie theaters to swoon over the Rock Hudson, Burt Lancaster, and Clark Gable types. Their hearts fluttered when Rhett Butler told Scarlett O'Hara, "Frankly, my dear, I don't give a damn." Now women tell men who don't live up to their standards, "Frankly, mister, I don't give a damn."

One thing will never change, however: survival of the fittest. Huntresses are programmed to prefer men who match Darwin's definition "best adapted for survival in the immediate, local environment."[26] Today, however, the "immediate local environment" is dramatically different. Now the crucial survival qualities are cooperation, compassion, curiosity, kindness, competitiveness, and an open mind.

Evolutionary psychologists who recognize that there are physiological spurts would call these "neo-Darwinian" qualities. The field encompassing that, developmental evolution, recognizes that the social environment changes in spurts, not at an even pace like evolutionists used to think.[27]

In the twenty-first century something new has been added to a woman's wish list. She wants intellectual growth and to reach her full potential as a person and a professional. A Huntress seeks a partner who will be supportive and help her accomplish that.

Hunters, even for ladies who are just looking for one-night nookie, your success and "good dad" indicators are what shoot brief spikes of voltage through your Quarry's brain.[28] But don't fret if you aren't a candidate for a *Men's Health* cover with bulging biceps and deltoids on steroids. This isn't to say that a woman doesn't like a really ripped guy—but only if it's attached to the right brain and attitude.[29]

Hunters, when is the last time you strutted into a bar and said to yourself, "Dude, tonight I am going to look so cooperative, compassionate, curious, kind, competitive, and show how supportive I am of a woman's personal growth that chicks will be lining up to meet me?" (Stay tuned, aspiring studs. You'll learn how to do that in the next section.) In short, a woman's looks are the first thing a man notices.[30] A man's character and personality are number one on a woman's most wanted in a partner list.[31]

Now we come to the most alluring physical quality for both sexes. It's one we seldom think of.

Planet Earth's Colossal Unisex Chemistry Sparker

Having a symmetrical face and body is like winning the lottery in attraction for both Hunters and Huntresses the world over because it screams "healthy genes."[32] You and I could see a good gene sitting next to a bad one on a plate, and it wouldn't say anything to us. But dump a batch of good ones into one baby and you'll see a big difference. Each tiny toe on his left foot looks exactly like the same one on the right. His little ears are mirror images of each other. Yet few would be conscious of its draw. Have you ever heard a woman swoon, "Honey, your symmetrical nose drives me wild"? Or a guy brag, "Dude, she's got the most balanced eyebrows I've ever seen"?

When you look at most faces, you think, "Sure, that's symmetrical." But I'm talking precise symmetry to the millimeter that only a fortunate one-tenth of 1 percent of the population has. If it's off one iota, it makes a difference. And it's not just perfectly balanced *faces*. We're talking symmetrical legs, shoulders, hips, thighs, fingers, elbows, breasts—and yes, even both sides of "it." Mother Nature draws females to symmetrical types, even if it's for one-night stands— especially when they're ovulating![33] After all, she figures, even that one shot could result in another healthy earthling.

Symmetry is also a powerful beauty plus in reptiles, insects, birds, and mammals because good genes also do a better job of battling environmental pollutants and parasites. Any self-respecting female fruit fly wouldn't even consider a guy fruit fly with asymmetrical spiracles.

Symmetrical guys, go ahead and gloat because studies show:

1. you start having sex four years earlier than your more symmetry-challenged brothers;[34]
2. you get laid more often and have a greater number of partners throughout your lifespan;[35]
3. you smell better to women than your more uneven, asymmetrical competitors;[36] and
4. you will give your girlfriends more and better orgasms than the more lopsided chaps do.[37]

Huntresses, here is a warning for you. They may look great, but be careful about those super-symmetrical guys. Statistically, they are less apt to stay with one partner and have more extramarital affairs throughout their lives.[38] Also be extra vigilant if you don't want to get pregnant, because your vagina sucks up more sperm from the better orgasms that symmetrical Hunters give you.[39]

Cliff Notes

You'll see the reasoning behind the Sparkers in the next section, but for now let's tally the list of what pokes Chemistry and gets the opposite sex's hormones hopping.

Hunters . . .

The *what*: Your signs of health, mental strength, compassion, wit, and assets or potential for same.

The *why*: Healthy men produce babies with stronger immune systems. Compassionate men care for them. Mentally strong men solve problems for them. And men with money give both baby and mother a better lifestyle.

Huntresses . . .

The *what*: Your large breasts, full lips, smaller waist, shapely hips, rosy cheeks, clear eyes, unblemished skin, and shiny hair.

The *why*: All the above qualities reflect high estrogen, meaning he can impregnate you quicker for a healthier baby.

In short . . .

A man is attracted to a woman's ability to grow a baby inside her.

A woman is attracted to a man's ability to grow a baby outside him.

So now we know *what* charges the electrical fields in your Quarry's brain and *why*. Let's move on to the specific Chemistry Sparkers and *how* to set the traps for the Big Catch.

CHAPTER 3

How to Spark Chemistry to Attract

Let's say one Saturday you and a few friends decide to go fishing. You get some poles, pack a bucket of worms for bait, and head out to the local lake. Trout are leaping onto the hooks, and you all have a fabulous time. Everyone laughs and cheers as they make catch after catch. The guys take turns carrying the big basket of fish to a friend's country cabin. You open a case of beer, turn on some music, and cook a great trout dinner.

It was such a blast that you plan a repeat experience the next Saturday. With fishing rods over your shoulders and toting a bucket of minnows for bait this time, your group treks to the lake, humming all the way. Excitedly, you put your bait on the hook and cast off. Everyone waits for the fish to swarm toward them like the previous week.

An hour goes by. No bites. Hmm. Two hours pass. Still nothing. After three hours you all give up and get Chinese takeout on the way back to the cabin.

What went wrong? Those of you who fish probably know the answer. You used the wrong bait. Trout don't eat minnows.

Cut to a party. Now you're fishing for a bigger catch, someone to date, have sex with, love, and perhaps build a life with. Lots of attractive people are swimming around the bar and everybody is hoping for the best catch. But only a lucky few lovers succeed. Why doesn't the majority? They use the wrong bait.

Here's the right kind.

Forget the Golden Rule When Trying to Spark Chemistry

You've heard of the Golden Rule: *Do unto others as you would have them do unto you.* That's fine for most situations. But not for igniting that Spark at first sight. Forget the Golden Rule and use the Platinum Rule, which I'll explain shortly.

When a Huntress first spots a man, she is instinctively aware of his character, confidence, kindness, and demeanor. She hopes to find intelligence and humor. If she likes him, she wants respect from the gentleman from the first "hello." In the back of her mind she's wondering if a relationship might be in the future.

When a Hunter first spots a woman, he judges her looks and receptivity to him. In the front of his mind he's wondering if sex might be in the future—and how soon.

Using the Golden Rule—treat others as you'd like to be treated—to appeal to a Quarry is one of the most foolish and common mistakes that potential lovers make. Huntresses are especially guilty of this. Girlfriend, at this point a guy is not judging your character, kindness, intelligence, and how much of a lady you are. Later, for a serious relationship with you, your character and other fine qualities are all important to him. *But not at first.* Luring him with those aspects of your personality before the first "hello" is the wrong bait because most guys are not thinking beyond the bedroom.

Conversely, Hunters, she is. Your abs of steel and bulging biceps pale as bait compared to other qualities she craves in a man. Later, when the two of you are in a loving relationship, she'll long to lick your killer pecs and squeeze your muscles. *But not at first.* She's visualizing beyond the bedroom. In fact, unless you have the "beyond" qualities, there probably won't even be the bedroom. Sexiness is the wrong bait for a guy to cast because she's thinking possible relationship.

Chemistry Sparker #1

Use the Platinum Rule When Luring Quarry

When trying to entice your Quarry, do not "Do unto others as you would have them do unto you." Instead, "Do unto others as *they* would like to be done unto." Hunters, displaying your good-guy qualities and demonstrating respect for the lady is the best bait. Huntresses, sexiness and showing that you're receptive to him are what reels him in.

Fight, Flight, or Chemistry at First Sight?

I didn't name this segment "Eye Contact" lest you skip it. I understand. I probably would have too. Millions of magazines, newspapers, books, and blogs—including mine—have done the subject to death. That aside, I would be remiss not to address it first.

Continuing unbroken eye contact can cause even a small Spark to catch fire. In studies, opposite-sex strangers directed to have extended eye contact reported neurochemical reactions similar to romantic sentiments.[1] Additionally, eyes locked for a period of time can give the sense that you are already in love. The *Journal of Research in Personality* reported that people who are deeply in love gaze at each other 30 to 40 percent more than other couples do, and they are slower to look away during an intrusion.[2]

There's more. Maintaining enduring eye contact also gives you the cachet of being a wiser abstract thinker because confident and creative individuals integrate incoming data more easily than concrete thinkers. They can continue looking into someone's eyes even during the silences.[3]

Unfortunately, most writers make it sound like "eye contact" is simply staring into each other's eyeballs. No, plain old eye contact between a man and a woman is all too common to Spark your Quarry majorly on its own without a strong message emanating from your eyes. I'll give you a few ways to use those grenades over your nose to capture your Quarry. But, first, gentlemen . . .

Get Wise to the Geisha in Every Woman

Unfortunately, there is a lot of misunderstanding about what eye contact signifies. Here is an all-too-common scenario: Guy smiles at girl. Girl looks away. Guy thinks it's rejection. Girl is disappointed. End of story.

Most Western males think a female glancing away means she's not interested. Wrong! Japanese men don't fall for it. They know that the lady's little smile and demure downward glance is part of the game, the world-famous geisha ploy. Her shyly (or slyly) lowering gaze is part of the female International Courtship Ritual.

This eye contact edict has been in effect since the beginning of time. If you've seen the infamous painting, *The Fall of Man: Adam and Eve*, you'll observe that the first human Hunter is looking at his Quarry's eyes. But Eve is demurely gazing elsewhere, all the while enticing him with the forbidden apple.

Gentlemen, it's not *if* she looks away. She will. (Well, unless she's read this book.) It's *how* she does it that counts.[4] When you reward her with a smile, your Quarry will either . . .

1. *Modestly sweep her eyes down at the floor as though admiring the carpet.* Experienced and confident Hunters know this is standard operating procedure for a flirting female and is as good as an engraved invitation. Go introduce yourself.
2. *Turn away with her eyes parallel, like inspecting the wall's paint job.* She's thinking, "Hmm, I'll reserve my judgment on you until after our first chat. The probability is good if you pass the "chat test." Go for it.
3. *Look up and away like checking the ceiling for ugly cracks.* Here she might as well be rolling her eyes into the next state and your chances of victory are slim. But, hey, you never know. Make a move—but only if you're good at accepting rejection.

Gentlemen, here is another clue. After she looks away, if she glances back at you again within the minute, you must approach or else she'll be sorely disappointed.

Huntresses, Fight Your Instincts

Huntresses, if you are one of the vast majority of women who de-murely look away when a man smiles at you, it's not your fault. Nature programmed you that way a very long time ago. Cro-Magnon males loved the thrill of the chase, just like guys today. But his female Quarry's feigned modesty didn't bother him one bit because the out-come would be the same either way. The confident Cro-Magnon just kept marching toward her with his erect club. However, Mother Nature didn't factor on modern males becoming so insecure that they would interpret the ladies' looking down as rejection and give up.

Girl, do not look away. Gaze into his eyes, smile, and put down your book, drink, or anything else that a panicky Hunter could mistake as a warrior's brass shield. When he's within easy conversational distance, be the first to say "hi." You will hear his palpable sigh of relief.

Eye Contact Is Not Unisex

Hunters and Huntresses must use their eyes in diverse and complex tactical ways to keep the Chemistry churning. The following Sparker Number Two is for Hunters, Three and Four are for Huntresses, and Five for both.

APPRAISING EYES

For an attractive woman, being ogled is as common as hearing her own breath. A brief meeting of the eyes gives her no neural jolt—unless your eyes stay persistently on hers and say something special. Here's how. Upon spotting your Quarry, keep your eyes on her face, not with an all-too-common hungry smile but in a mode I call "ap-praising eyes" to give her a several-layer chemical rush.

I didn't comprehend what was happening to me at the time, but I now know I was the happy victim of that emotional tidal wave. At a dinner party I smiled at a distinguished gentleman near the end of the table. Apparently not noticing, he continued conversing with the lady on his left. When he tenderly touched her hand, I felt a jab of jealousy, assuming they were a couple.

Then, while drowning my disappointment in the bowl of soup, I felt his eyes on me. Looking up, I almost dropped my spoon. He was stroking his chin and staring at me through squinted eyes like a radiologist inspecting an x-ray. It lasted only a few seconds, but it gave me emotional vertigo. When a smile flooded his face, I felt like I'd been saved from the lions. I wouldn't have appreciated it had his attention been too quick. Metaphorically, if I'd been hooked up to an *f*MRI, the activity in my brain would have blown the circuits. Hunters, if you make it seem like she's earned your approval, she'll crave it all the more. Incidentally, the man at the end of the table was the ship's captain I mentioned earlier who is now my partner.

Chemistry Sparker #2

Don't Just Look At but "Appraise" Your Quarry

When she notices your gaze, don't give her the panting puppy dog smile that a lot of misguided guys do. Take charge and inspect her face like a jeweler appraising a valuable gem. Appear to be judging her demeanor, her disposition, her character, her comportment, her sensitivity, her soul, her whatever. Anything but her looks. The lady wants to feel that it was more than her beauty that caught your eye. Only after she sees you looking at her, let your lips form a slow smile of considered approval.

Huntresses, the next two are for you. In a sense the techniques are opposites.

Submissive Eyes

Males are instinctively super-sensitive to hostile aggression.[5] Even if you are only half his size, a Hunter could find your extremely intense eye contact threatening. When he glances your way, look straight into his eyes, but let yours express instant admiration and slight submissiveness.

You can give him an extra Spark with a ploy that has animal origins. When two foxes fight in the wilderness, the one that loses submits and bares his exposed neck to the knifelike teeth of the victor. This vulnerability is an exhilarating feeling for the latter. Give him the homosapien version of this "I submit to you" signal.

♀ Chemistry Sparker #3

Tilt Your Head and Caress Your Neck During Eye Contact

Huntresses, keep your eyes glued to his, but tilt your head to soften the exchange. Meanwhile, gently stroke your neck. Primal instinct tells him that you are protecting it because if it came to bloodshed, you know he'd win. It makes him feel like the masterful Hunter he imagines himself to be.

Daring Eyes

Be prepared, girl. Some of the following Chemistry-Sparking techniques are over the top and for gutsy Huntresses only. You must have the feminine version of brass balls to carry them off—and the skill to turn him around later during the first conversation. However, I want to make one thing perfectly clear: I am *not* suggesting you have loose morals or be less than the lady you are. I am *not* suggesting you jump into bed with him any time soon. But you must lure him sexually so he can discover the real you. Casting the correct bait, then reeling in your Quarry, require two very different skill sets.

♀ Chemistry Sparker #4

Scan His Body Shamelessly with Your Eyes

As your eyes meet, let yours travel south. Start at his shoulders, work your way down his chest, then linger a second on his belt. (Courageous Huntresses, go a bit farther.) Explore his body top to crotch like an airport security officer inspecting a passenger in a body scanner.

When you've finished your scrutiny, swiftly look up into his eyes and reward him with your smiling seal of approval.

Needless to say, gentlemen, for the sake of your freedom, do not attempt this on her. You do not need a police report on your record. The next Sparker is for both sexes and makes you feel a connection at the first meeting of the eyes.

LOVING EYES

Do you remember we talked about how the people who surrounded an infant in the first five years form a great part of the person's LoveMap? As a child, your Quarry's parents' eyes expressed unconditional love—watching her sleeping in the crib, taking her first step, wobbling on his first bicycle ride, putting a bandage on his scraped knee. When he was a baby, he felt the love in Mommy's eyes while holding him. She sensed the adoration in Daddy's when he made funny faces to entertain her.

Have you heard people say, "She has loving eyes," or "I could see the love in his eyes?" It's true. That deep emotion does show in a person's eyeballs because internal thoughts produce physiological responses that your observer is subliminally aware of.[6] So physiologically, you can come a step nearer to fitting your Quarry's LoveMap with this self-talk technique. To those of you who think the following Sparker is too far-fetched or "touchie-feelie," I invite you to view the part of any video in which lovers fall in love at first sight. Press the pause button at the second their eyes meet. Now study all four eyes looking at their soon-to-be beloved and you'll see their pupils are ever so slightly enlarged.

Chemistry Sparker #5

Give Your Quarry "Family Eyes"

While maintaining eye contact, repeat to yourself, "I feel you're like my family and therefore I love you." That automatically enlarges your pupils and softens your eyes, making them even more attractive and inviting. It simulates the admiration, acceptance, and unconditional love that your Quarry basked in as a child.[7]

I said earlier that Hunters and Huntresses should use their eyes in different ways to attract Quarry. Consider that a gross understatement when it comes to using your body, personality, and clothes. I flipped a coin to see which sex's strategy we'd explore first. Heads, Hunters. Tails, Huntresses.

Heads won.

Hunters' Fishing Trip

Pickup Artists, or PUAs, as men on the prowl proudly refer to themselves, dig sexy women. So it's understandable that many misguided men assume "sexy" is near the top of a woman's wish list. But when was the last time you think a woman said, "Hey girlfriend, I sure would like to meet that hairy half-naked stud over there who looks like his jeans were put on with a spray can?" (That only happens on some TV so-called reality shows.) Guys have a hard time getting it into their heads that the female brain is totally different from theirs. Keep in mind that her hormones intuitively respond to qualities like compassion, confidence, consideration, intelligence, and financial security.[8]

"Okay," you are saying, "if I hear you correctly, these are qualities I can prove to her when we start talking and dating. But what's that got to do with her feeling quick Chemistry with me? I can't just go up to a chick and say, 'Hi, I'm caring, kind, clever, loaded with capital, can coach you to achieve your full potential, and be a great dad. Can I buy you a drink?' I mean, she doesn't even know me yet."

Oh yes she does! Compared to you, a female is a clairvoyant with x-ray vision. She senses more about you in a split second than you can in an hour of gaping at her. There are three main reasons:

1. A female's neurons are more densely crowded in certain layers of the cortex that are responsible for signals coming

in and out of the brain, so they have enhanced communication with each other—and with subtleties in the outside world.[9]

2. A woman also has ten times more "white matter" in her brain—and that's where she does a lot of her thinking. The significance of that? Neurons in white matter have more connections between them and have something like a greased tube called a *myelin sheath*.[10] This makes her interbrain signals even quicker. Compare it to the clarity of a land line versus a cell phone.

3. The connection between a female's left brain (logical and analytical) and right brain (intuitive and subjective) is stronger.[11] That means she can put you under a microscope to examine your every expression, every gesture, and every syllable for its significance. Even what it revealed about you when you asked the bartender for more peanuts.

She's probably given you the thumbs up or cast you to the lions before you take your first step toward her, so from her first glance, you must demonstrate that you are an evolved twenty-first-century-kinda guy.

Your Actions Speak Louder Than Looks

Let's say you're at a Looking-4-Luv singles bar, and of course, the women are furtively checking you out. (It's a fact. Women who are single and searching check out every man who enters the room.[12]) Gentlemen, carefully visualize yourself doing the following and then we'll analyze the coolness of your strategy step by step.

You are well dressed, pause in the doorway, survey the situation, and pretend not to notice your Quarry. You enter at a smooth pace, and as you head toward the bar, a couple of guys give you a fist bump. Then you greet a buddy and slap him on the back. Asking the bartender for a beer, he smiles and chats with you while two women try unsuccessfully to catch your eye. Then an attractive girl you obviously know approaches. When you whisper something in her ear, she laughs and you brush a hair off her cheek. You then put an arm around her shoulder and the two of you continue talking with your friends.

The reason your moves are Sparking her pleasure center (or caudate nucleus) is because this brain region has a tendency to live somewhat in the future. It fantasizes kicks–to-come more than it pictures the joys of the present.[13] She's instinctively and subconsciously imagining you playing a future role in her life.

Gentlemen, one by one, let's go over the dozen super-cool moves you made.

1. *You dressed well.*
   The lady likes that. She knows good clothes will travel further in the business world than ripped jeans do.

2. *You paused and looked around with a friendly expression.*
   That makes you look kind. If you come across as tough, Mother Nature nudges her, "Watch out, dear, he might be ruthless to you and the family someday!"

3. *You strolled in at a smooth pace.*
   Your walk evidences a strong immune system. If you limp into the room like a centipede with ninety-six missing legs, your uneven gait could signal a weak one. Huntresses pick up on the scent of bad genes like the smell of a dead mouse under the refrigerator.

4. *You didn't appear to notice her.*

   That was a very cool move. It made you look like you weren't on the prowl.

5. *A couple of guys gave you the fist bump.*

   A man needs supportive colleagues to get ahead so having male friends is a big plus to women.[14]

6. *You greeted a buddy and slapped him on the back.*

   Excellent. That displays friendly dominance. Think about it, an employee doesn't slap his employer's back. A slave doesn't slap his master's back. It's the other way around. In other words, the slapper is "on top."

7. *The bartender smiled and chatted with you.*

   His respect proves you have a good reputation in that establishment.

8. *Two women looked at you flirtatiously.*

   You are more of a prize if other women want you.[15]

9. *An attractive girl approached you.*

   "Uh oh," you might think. "My Quarry might assume that's my girlfriend, that I'm 'taken.'" Not a problem, gentlemen. It's okay to give her a little scare because it triggers fearful electrochemical activity in her amygdala. In a perverse way, however, she gets a kick out of it, like a scary movie.

   Besides, if you're in a relationship with a woman, that means you are "preapproved." It's like buying a string of pearls at a yard sale versus a reputable antique store. At the yard sale you're taking a chance. In the antique store they're probably the real McCoy.

10. *You whispered something in the woman's ear and she laughed.*

    That evidenced your good sense of humor. In Chapter 6 you'll learn some surprising reasons why women like men who make them laugh.[16]

11. *You brushed a hair off her cheek.*

    That was a killer move. Mother Nature tells her "Girl, this guy is the protective sort and will take care of you and the kids."

12. *Then you put your arm around her.*

That is a male version of "playing hard to get." The jealousy gene bites and kicks your Quarry's competitive juices into action. Here's one that's in *Ripley's Believe It or Not*, or at least "Leil's Believe It or Not." I didn't until I read the studies. Most women don't mind doing what sociologists call "mate poaching."[17] Researchers asked women at Oklahoma State if they would actively pursue a man with qualities matching her wish list. Fifty-nine percent said yes. Then they asked, "What if the man was already in a committed relationship?" This time 90 percent of the women said they would go after him![18]

Let's sum it up. You've given the lady's pleasure center hints of good things to come with your smell of success, good genes, sense of humor, respect from other men, and caring qualities. Then you gave her brain an electrical jolt of fear that you're taken. Now when you approach your Quarry, she will be fully primed.

Chemistry Sparker #6

Don't Act "Hot." Act "Cool Dad."

Hunters, in preparing for your next pursuit, the key words are not "sexy hot" or even "handsome." Think "caring." Think "coach." Think "kind," think "clever," think "capital." Think— are you ready?—"cool dad." I know it's impossible to replicate the previous scenario, but squeeze in as many elements as possible to give tiny Sparks to any woman watching you.

Smiling Is Not Just Smiling

When the usual horny Hunter smiles at a woman, his objective is as obvious as a tarantula on his lips. You must show that you are different. I discovered the perfect expression to accomplish that while watching a teenager at a playground with his little sister. He obviously adored her and seldom took his eyes off her. I'll never forget the warm, protective look on his face as he helped her climb the precarious jungle gym. I call it the "Little Sister Smile." Use the following visualization technique.

Chemistry Sparker #7

Bestow the "Little Sister Smile" on Your Quarry

Let your mind play a trick on your lips. When you first spot her, visualize a vulnerable someone you love and want to protect at all costs as you would a little sister. Your caring smile instinctively warms her heart and sets you apart from "all those other animals" with their leering grins.

Does She Really Care What I Wear?

In a word, "Yes!" To her, your clothes are a projection of who you are.[19] Never lose sight of the fact that a woman reads something into everything. Unlike you, she doesn't have sex-ray vision to undress her Quarry mentally. No matter what you think, she is not salivating to see the bulging biceps and washboard abs beneath your threads. She loves a great body but prefers it covered until impending intimacy.[20]

In an infamous research project called the "Hamburger Study," women saw photos of guys ranging from Tom Cruise look-alikes down to pictures of men even the photographer would be afraid to be alone with in the studio.[21] The women didn't know the photos were of the same guys, sometimes wearing suits, sometimes in Burger King uniforms. Many of the former were chosen as "husband material," but none of the poor fast-food slingers. Yes, a male's hunting gear is important to make the kill. To a woman, a well-dressed male is a bigger turn-on than an almost-naked one.[22]

When I was cruise director on a ship, the waiters were all Italian and gorgeous. At the grand finale dinner on the last night, we had a surprise tradition. Suddenly all the lights would go out. Just as passengers were freaking over a power outage, the music blared out. A hundred drop-dead gorgeous, sizzling waiters marched out of the kitchen wearing only tiny Speedo bathing suits and carrying candle-decorated baked Alaska above their shoulders.

The women hooted. The girls screamed. The men closed their eyes. Everyone laughed hysterically. The women told me they thought it was hilarious—but not a turn-on.

Conversely, Hunters, if you saw a parade of practically naked beauties carrying cakes with candles above their heads, your eyeballs would jump out and dangle by the optic nerve. Even if you were starving, you wouldn't even notice the cake.

Why Coordinated Clothes Counts

Sometimes, when my housemate Phil dresses for a date, he asks me how he looks. I break it to him gently, but I don't dare let him go out in his brown Timberland boots with navy pants and an olive, short-sleeved shirt. (Gentlemen, even if it's hot as a jet's exhaust outside, do not sport short sleeves. It short-circuits your sex appeal. Go for long sleeves rolled up.)

Think "coordinated." No black slacks with brown shoes; no brown belt with black shoes; no black socks with olive pants. And, horror of horrors, no piece of hairy leg showing in between. That merits you a female's "yuck" every time.

You've heard rumors that women always notice your shoes. Well, kill the rumor and file it under fact. Some have an uncanny ability to spot a pair of Pradas attached to the bottom of a male sitting on the other side of a crowded party. Buy one quality pair of shoes for your hunting expeditions.

"Why does the female population care about what I wear?" you ask. Because coordinated clothes demonstrate creativity, taste, and intelligence. Perhaps you're thinking, "But the kind of women I want wouldn't care about such surface stuff." Don't be so sure! Even the waitress from the One Horse Coffee Shop, who has never been out-side of the town it's named after, has an uncanny sense of the quality of your clothes.

Chemistry Sparker #8

Dress Like You're Auditioning to Be Her Husband

Make sure your threads are good quality and soft because females are more sensitive to touch than you.[23] Think quality, not quantity. And neatness counts. Even though the other guys might think it's cool to go out dressed like an unmade bed, set yourself apart. You can be casual, of course, but be casual chic, not casual cheap.

Don't sweat it if your budget is more beer than champagne. Run the numbers. A small closet of fine-quality clothes costs a fourth of all the junk you most likely have stashed in it now. Unlike women, you can wear the same outfit more often—as long as you air it out every now and then.

A final tidbit: Before the big date that you're hoping will end with her asking "Your place or mine?" you have a tough decision. Boxers or briefs? Brief briefs or full briefs? Plain boxers or bright boxers? Colored briefs or white briefs?

There are no referenced studies for the following, but the results of the "Official Dr. Lowndes Seminar Participants Survey" says women prefer good-quality, low-cut white or black briefs on a man. But not too brief.

Huntresses' Fishing Trip

Huntresses, now it's your turn to embark on the Quarry safari at the same location, the Looking-4-Luv singles spot. Let's say, because you are drop-dead gorgeous, you know men will soon swoop down on you like seagulls fighting over a crumb. But naturally you don't want just any ol' male sidling up to you, saying, "What's a pretty girl like you doing in a place like this?" You deserve a gentleman. So to attract more refined Quarry, you take a ladylike position and cross your legs daintily. Oops, your skirt rides up. A few men glance your way and you shyly look down. Another nice-looking man smiles at you. You quickly pull your skirt down lest he think you're cheap. When you look up again, he's chatting up some overly made-up hussy who is way less good looking than you. What an animal!

Another cool guy glances your way. As you demurely rearrange your blouse, he goes back to talking to his buddy. Ten minutes go by, and a few other Hunters smile at you. You sweetly look away and await their approach.

But it never happens! Why didn't any of them come over to say, "hi"? Not one of them offered to buy you a drink. You're thinking, "I could be lying on the floor gasping for breath, dying of thirst, and no one would care." You figure every man in the bar is either blind, gay, or with a jealous girlfriend who packs a pistol in her purse.

What Went Wrong?

No one approached because, when you sat down, your body looked like it was wearing a "Private Property" or "Keep Out" sign. When one gentleman glanced your way, you went into the archaic geisha act. Another stole a peek at your knees and you hid them. Then you modestly rearranged your blouse so guys couldn't see your alluring neckline.

Do you really think a guy will tell his buddy, "Hey Bro, think I'll go make a move on that prim little lady over there who turned away and hid her knees from me?" To any woman who wants to capture the "grand slam," as animal hunters call the biggest and the best of each species, I'm saying "Girl, you have to change your stalking style!" All the studies prove it: Friendly slightly suggestive aggressiveness is the name of the game if you want to win.

How the "Beauty Challenged" Can Ace the "Tens"

Huntresses, earlier we talked about the extraordinary importance of looks. So one would logically assume that most men, spotting both an attractive woman and a plain one at a party, would approach the former. This is not true!

Using the common one-to-ten beauty-scale measurement, researchers engaged courageous young women of average attractiveness to go to pubs where singles mingle and to flirt overtly with men they didn't know. During all the activity the eagle-eyed investigators feverishly took notes on cocktail napkins, tracking which women various men approached—the gorgeous women or the average-looking ladies in the experiment. Their findings?

If you are friendly and obviously flirtatious, men are more apt to approach you than they are the most gorgeous women in the room. But don't just take my word for it. Enjoy all the delicious details in any of dozens of studies. They are a thrilling read for us single-digit gals.[24]

A Hunter's Brain Is Like a Light Switch with a Delayed Connection

You've felt that instant Spark just spotting a guy on the street. Sure, guys can feel that too, *if* the lady fits his previously established LoveMap. Perhaps she has just the right face, precise body, and DNA to invoke those scillions of pleasurable subconscious associations. But if you're not that one in a million, all is not lost. You can still give his brain brief spikes of voltage that he'll swear was an "instant" Spark. Why? Because the male neural "instant" is longer than yours due to those slower neurotransmissions and lack of lubricated myelin sheaths in his gray matter. His relative sluggishness on interpersonal subtleties is excellent news when trying to Spark Chemistry because you have time to flip his switch before the male "instant" is up. You toggle it by doing something suggestive.

Sisters, I'm assuming your first interest in meeting your Quarry is not just sex but also a possible relationship. You want him to be interested in you as a person, not a sex object. But of course, his first interest *is* sex! So why shouldn't *you* do what you expect *him* to do for you? The Platinum Rule, remember? Don't approach him with *your* interests in mind. Approach him with *his*. In other words, lure your Quarry with hints of sex—then capture him with your substantial qualities.

For us women, it's just the opposite. We like a guy and, when we recognize his fine qualities, we become all the more sexually interested in him. But for a man, the sexual excitement must be there first. We'll talk about that now—then we'll get to turning him around. A little later I'll give you techniques to show him that you are most definitely not just a sex object and dozens of ways to win his respect and love.

Hunting Gear for Trapping First-Class Quarry

In light of what I wrote in the "body parts" paragraphs in Chapter 2, you have every right to assume I'll suggest you dress seductively.

Absolutely not! My Granny was no fool. Her words are as true today as when I was a teen. Once, as I was proudly spinning around, showing off my new micro-miniskirt, she took my hand and cautioned, "Leilie, there are two kinds of girls in this world. The marrying kind and 'the other kind.'" I rolled my eyes.

This many years later I owe her an apology. All serious studies support her wisdom. Instead of Granny's very unacademic designation of "the other kind," however, researchers call them females with "short-term mating strategies" or "munificent" women.[25] Yes, I had to look that word up too. It means "bountiful," "willing to give gifts," "generous." Seeing her in too much makeup and too few clothes, no one needs to ask what she's generous with.

We've all seen guys at parties or at the mall salivating over these short-term-strategy ladies. But not one of those panting males would invite a woman with Cleopatra makeup and cleavage to her navel to his company's Christmas party. So tone down the makeup and torch the scanty outfit that you store in a matchbox. That gets you a large *quantity* of attention, but not *quality* attention.

I told Hunters about the quality and fashion of their clothes. What about yours? Do men make judgments about that? Absolutely not. The coordination, the cost, how it reflects your deep, inner qualities, how much money you make, and whether your outfit augurs well for your future together is lambda calculus to them. In research similar to the Hamburger Study, men viewed women wearing everything from designer garb to bag-lady clothes.[26] Men always chose the good-looking females even if they were sporting Salvation Army rejects. It doesn't matter what you wear; it's the little tricks you'll soon learn about using your clothes that count.

Forget Fashion, Think Flirtation

Naturally, you should match the intensity of the following techniques to your personality, the venue, the class, and the presumed mindset of your Quarry. But do not match them to your "comfort level." Unless you are a hooker on heroin, I guarantee your comfort level is far too low. You'll have plenty of time later to demonstrate you are not a woman of easy virtue or "that kind of girl." If you want a long-term relationship with him, you must start doing that during the first conversation.

A Hunter doesn't notice your clothing, but he certainly notices what he sees of your body. That's where "adjustable clothing" comes in. Dress conservatively but in clothes you can shift around to reveal a little more of your body to *only* your target man. An example is a soft blouse with a scoop neck that you can tug revealingly to the side

to show more skin. Alternatively, you can let your blouse "acciden-
tally" slip off one shoulder when he looks your way. Or a full skirt
you can slide up to show more leg. Incidentally, here's a model's trick
to make your legs shapelier when you do. With your legs crossed,
push the calf of your top calf out with your bottom knee. Try it now
and you'll see what I mean.

If a man's testosterone shoots up by a third just talking to an attractive woman, can you imagine how it skyrockets when you gently
tug at your attire to expose a tad more of yourself? Getting a glimpse
of even a relatively "innocent" part of your body like a thigh, a naked
shoulder, or even a bare foot when you dangle a shoe on your toes
gives him a little Spark—and they all add up to a big one.

♀ Chemistry Sparker #9

Don't Wear Revealing Clothes.
Wear "Adjustable" Ones

Don't reveal cleavage or too much leg that any guy in the
vicinity could gape at. Instead, sport outwardly conservative
clothing that you can shift and slide around to reveal only
what you want, *when* you want, and *how* you want to excite
the *who* you want. Make it obvious that your ministrips are
solely for your Quarry's viewing pleasure alone.

By the way, here's a neuroanatomical heads up: Don't waste your
artillery more than forty degrees to his right or left during any of
these maneuvers. A Hunter has fewer receptor rods and cones in his
retina, so his peripheral vision is narrower.[27] Stand as close as you
can to his direct line of vision whenever casting bait.

Sizzling Sparkers for Serious Huntresses

I learned this scorching Sparker in college. Not in class but from a petite brunette who had just moved into my dorm. Shannon was sweet but shy—the reserved, quiet type. So we were all shocked when Carson, the Big Catch on Campus, who had only dated hot women, fell for her.

Late one Saturday night after she and I had both returned from dates, I walked into the dorm's community shower room. Shannon was just slipping out of her dress revealing—I gasped—a skimpy, black lace garter belt, stockings, and a see-through bra! Embarrassed, she threw a towel around herself and scurried back to her room.

Sitting on the shower bench struggling to remove my tight pantyhose, I instantly realized what Carson saw in her. She was the type of girl he'd be proud to introduce to his family. Yet underneath, Shannon obviously was sexually savvier than any of his previous hot dates.

I thought that was pretty cool and made it a point to become her friend to see what else I could learn. On our way to lunch one time we passed a Victoria's Secret lingerie store. I asked if she wanted to stop in.

"Why, Leil?" Then I teased her about her sizzling undergarments.

"Laugh all you like," she said. "It works."

"I'm sure it does, Shannon. And you go strutting around the campus in hot sexy underwear for all the guys to enjoy, ha ha!"

"No!" Taking mock offense, she continued, "I'm very particular who gets to see it. In fact, that's how I met Carson." She looked around and lowered her voice. "I knew he always had lunch at the campus canteen, so one day I sat at another table directly across from him. Then, pretending I didn't notice, I let the top of my garter show. Naturally, he looked over, and when he did, I winked at him before hiding it. Of course he came over and said 'hi.'"

"Shannon, you've got to be kidding!"

"No, I am dead serious!"

"Girlfriend, you are one sassy lady! And when we met, I thought you were so shy."

"Not in all ways," she said coyly.

Sisters, it all has to do with your Quarry getting a private peek at the sexy forbidden, especially if you're revealing it especially for him. In the late nineteenth century savvy women in floor-length skirts flashed ankle. You need to raise the bar on this antiquity to just above your knees. Many men have told me that they find "the peek" at something usually hidden more exciting than nudity. Purposefully revealing a touch of a black garter or the top of a red lace bra says, "I may look conservative outside. But on the inside I'm bitchin' hot *just for you."*

♀ Chemistry Sparker #10

Look Sedate on the Outside, but Reveal Something Sizzling Underneath

When you're around small game, turn your body away, pull down your skirt, and button up your blouse. But when you spot your grand slam Quarry, reveal something sexy you are wearing underneath like the top of a lacy bra. It gives him a chock-full-of-testosterone Spark.

I highly suggest garters and stockings because a man seldom sees them in the twenty-first century except in hot magazines. The somewhat uncomfortable but very sexy contraptions have come a long way since Granny's day. They now spell s-e-x.

Take another tip from Shannon and put a touch of humor in your microstrip show. Your smile can express, "I know you know what I'm doing and I'm having fun. Hope you are too." Winks work wonderfully during your self-presentation. The beauty of this ocular flutter is your later claim, "What wink? I had something in my eye." (And you did—him.)

One Huntress's Triple-X Tip

I can't in all good conscience put my seal of approval on this next one, but I do have evidence of its efficacy. Again I'd like to repeat, in no way whatsoever should you come across as cheap. But you can conspire with Mother Nature to bag your Quarry quickly. A clever girl in one of my dating seminars came up with an ingenious little trick. During the coffee break several men were surrounding a particular young lady who was quite poised, well spoken, and dressed in a medium-length skirt and a silk turtleneck. There was nothing cheap about her. I remember being pleased at my male students' good taste.

When the class reconvened I asked participants to place their nametags higher on their right shoulders so I could see them from the podium. At that point I noticed Brittany's breasts—not large, but tipped with little BB-like protrusions.

Before the break I had asked the group to write attraction techniques anonymously on a card, which, with their permission, I would later read to the class. When I got to Brittany's card, my jaw dropped. I looked up and saw the demure little lady grinning as wide as a banana. She squeezed her lips together signaling, "Shh, it's our secret." The class was understandably confused when I broke out laughing.

Gentlemen, please skip the following. It's just a fashion tip (pun intended) for the ladies. Here's what Brittany had written on her card:

⚲ Chemistry Sparker #11

"Modify" Your Bra

"Leil, please don't use my name if you read this to the class, but here's a technique that works like magic. Whenever I'm going somewhere there might be interesting guys, I dress conservatively but I snip the tips off my bras so the shape of my nipples shows under my blouse."

The class had no idea why I was laughing as I tucked the card away.

Like all erotica, Mother Nature is behind the nipple magnetism for men.[28] During sex your nipples become firmer, and when you're nursing, the area expands. Big nipples also help your baby find lunch. So girl, if you weren't blessed with protruding nipples, take a tip from Brittany. Big Mama in the sky would even give you the shears!

Erotic Truth Is Stranger than Fiction

You've probably never consciously thought about it—nor has he— but a male is aroused by the scent of female underarms, therefore, also the sight of a lady's pits. As a further draw, Big Mama even makes them even spicier when you're ovulating.[29]

Napoleon, in his famous love letters to Josephine, wrote of the "intoxicating pleasures" of being with her. In one, he beseeched, "I am arriving in Paris in three days. Don't wash."

This one sounds too silly to merit a specific Sparker, so just consider it a hint. If you are wearing a sleeveless top, lift your arm and pretend to be arranging the back of your hair. He's too far away to actually sniff your pheromones, but it invokes sweet subliminal memories of other times his nose has nuzzled that usually unseen female territory.

THE OVULATING WALK

In the 1600s, a young orphan named Catherine commissioned a cobbler to craft a pair of shoes with a higher heel in the back. This had the effect of arching her back, thrusting out her buttocks and bosom, and putting a wiggle in her walk. (Not so incidentally, Catherine de' Medici managed to bag the future king of France at the age of fourteen.) Marilyn Monroe also took hip swinging seriously. Rumor has it that she shaved down one heel of all her stilettos to put a swing in her stride.

However, we're talking about a different gait that is more subtly sexually appealing than a wiggling walk or swinging stride. The best way to describe it would be an "undulating, very slow-motion gallop." The study, "Differences in Gait Across the Menstrual Cycle and Their Attractiveness to Men," demonstrated that women unconsciously dress more provocatively, and walk in this more sensuous manner during her big "O" days.[30] Mother Nature knows its power and programmed it into the walk of ovulating women to signal males that "it's time for you to make your move on me."

Ladies, don't be scandalized by some of the previous techniques. In Chapter 5, I will give you proof that if you handle your Quarry strategically in the ways I suggest, the blend of his weaker memory for details plus his stronger male ego will make him think he initiated the entire encounter. In fact, it's proven that females initiate two-thirds of all marriages, be it a smile, a come-hither look, or the first hello.[31]

Obviously you should tailor your tricks to your desired catch. Refined Quarry or someone residing on Easy Street might be turned off by techniques that would excite a guy living on the other side of the tracks, and vice versa. But even if your Quarry is sitting on the top of the invisible class totem pole, you can use potent soft-x techniques to Spark him.

♀ Chemistry Sparker #12

Do the Undulating Ovulating Walk When He's Watching

The next time you're ovulating (around midpoint between your period) take note of how your walk instinctively changes. Or view a video of a high-fashion model in skyscraper heels swiveling her skeleton butt on the catwalk. Then practice, practice, practice. Just don't walk that way at church or work. It's for "special occasions" only, like when your Quarry is watching you.

CHAPTER *4*

How to Spark Cyber Chemistry

When first introduced, online dating was a hush-hush humiliation for the pioneering few who clandestinely indulged in it. During that primitive period of romance, I remember asking one happy couple where they'd met. After an anxious change of glances, the wife nervously sputtered, "Well, it was, er, umm, at . . . " Her quick-thinking husband squeezed her hand and deftly jumped in, "Oh, I happened to see her picture and knew immediately I had to meet her." He didn't say where he'd seen it! Now, however, online dating is standard operating procedure for finding love and may soon be responsible for the majority of meetings. When today's babies reach teenhood, they might ask, "What were singles' bars?"

If the term *computer dating* still holds cringe-worthy associations for you, tell your hippocampus to banish the bad connotations. Dating sites are not just populated by cave trolls. Millions of single, divorced, and widowed fabulous folks are sincere love seekers just like you, and it may be just a click away.

Because information on writing a profile is plastered all over the web, and I promised to give you information that is found in few, if any, other places, I'll concentrate primarily on your picture. That's where the Chemistry starts.

The Successful Online Hunter

Gentlemen, a Huntress studies your face on the screen through her crystal ball to unearth what type of guy you are. Because she'll read between the lines on your face, choose a photo that shows character, not just a handsome guy. If wisdom is her big turn-on, she'll search for intelligence in your eyes. If she values a sense of humor, she'll look for credible laugh lines, not just a grimace for the camera. In the "Truth Is Stranger Than Fiction" category, researchers found that women can determine whether a guy wants kids just by looking at a picture of his face![1]

A good haircut is a big draw. You don't need to go to a stylist who charges by the follicle, but forget your neighborhood barber who moonlights as a butcher. The *Journal of Social Behavior and Personality* discovered that glasses can be an asset for men.[2] When asked why, women responded, "They make him look more intelligent." The female mind doesn't stop there. Glasses are also a "fashion statement." Are your frames up to date, meaning are you an *au courant* type of guy? Are they the right ones for your facial shape, meaning are you smart enough to make the right choices in life?

And, of course, your skin must scream "good genes." Gentlemen, here's a "You've got to be kidding" moment, but hang in there. To prove to her that you've got all-class genes, furtively slip into the cosmetic aisle of a drugstore to buy a gooey skin-colored product called "concealer." Just before the photo, lock your bathroom door and smear concealer on any pimples, rashes, broken capillaries, canker sores, large pores, or any other blight on your otherwise perfect face. (Do you think there is a newscaster, actor, or rock star alive who doesn't wear a little guy-liner while facing a camera or crowd?)

Four photos are optimal. More, you look vain. Less, the ladies can't see enough to make a considered choice. Final caution: Never post a self-taken shot of you in the bathroom mirror. That says, "I don't have a friend in the world, not even one I can talk into taking my picture."

Hunters' Clothes

Gentlemen, your garb represents a possible future lifestyle to your Quarry. Does she see herself on the arm of a business tycoon in a suit, a surgeon in scrubs, a jock in a football uniform, or a casual fun-loving guy in jeans? Give the lady fodder for her fantasies.

If you select the "I'm a nice, regular guy" image, which is probably the best choice, follow the guidelines in Chapter 3 on clothing. The whole "ensemble" should look casually coordinated, perhaps a bit costly. Depending on your age and lifestyle, gentlemen, one shot in a suit doesn't hurt. It makes you look more successful professionally.

Yes, gentlemen, the job in your profile makes big difference.[3] To cover your bets, unless you have controlling interest in all creation, some men told me they had more success listing a generic category (i.e., "business," "the arts," etc.) than stating their specific job. Some of you really hot-looking dudes might be asking, "What about one shirtless shot showing my rippling muscles and ripped abs?" No, that is way beyond cheesy as a choice. Your biceps may show success at the gym, but she's more interested in your success in life. She figures it's better that her future kids have a bright daddy than a beefcake daddy.

Hunters' Background

You may not be aware of it, but Huntresses also scrutinize every megapixel of what's behind you in your picture. Your surroundings can make her respond/delete decision.[4] What's in the background of your outdoor shot? A battered truck, a motorcycle, a Subaru, or a Mercedes? What about an indoor shot? For some picky Huntresses, the click/no-click decision comes down to curtains, blinds, or stark-naked dirty windows. Whatever is in the background, she's pondering, "Would I like to live there or ride in that?"

It doesn't hurt to have another woman in a secondary shot, but only if she's stunning. A study called, "The Effects of Having a Physically Attractive Partner on Person Perception" confirmed that when a man has a dazzling woman in tow, the world considers him richer, more accomplished, and better looking.[5] If you decide to go this route, make sure that *all* of the woman shows, not part of her cropped out. I've seen some pretty lame photos of Hunters with a woman's hand on his arm, and the rest of her sliced off. Your Quarry subconsciously fears that the next woman he slices out of his life will be her. Alas, our gentle sex reads something into everything.

Chemistry Sparker #13

Photo Tips: Show Character in Your Face and Have an Appealing Background

Make sure the lighting shows character and depth in your face and that you're not "just another good looking guy." Don't forget the touch of concealer to signal, "I have good genes." Pay extra attention to the background to make her feel, "I'd like to be there with you."

The Successful Online Huntress

Girl, let's say a Hunter writes you a cool message. You write an even cooler one back. You text a bit and then plan to talk. So far, so good. Visions of romance and maybe happily-ever-after dance through your head.

But stop. None of these pleasures will be part of your future if he doesn't like your cyber image. It's no news to women that their picture is the primary—probably only—factor that encourages a Hunter to click on their profiles.[6] My only ubiquitous recommendation is to make sure it is recent and resembles you somewhat. I mention that merely because a male student in one of my relationship seminars told me that while waiting in a restaurant to meet his online date, a woman vaguely resembling the lady's picture walked through the restaurant door. He assumed she had sent her mother to apologize for her daughter being unable to keep the date. The rest of the men laughed knowingly. Obviously they had suffered a similar experience.

My regular readers may remember that, for a short while, I ran a modeling agency, and my girls gave me two great photo tips. First, the world's most photographed women close their eyes for a few seconds between camera clicks to magnify their pupils, making them more attractive. Second, a professional model doesn't "suck" in her tummy before the camera clicks. She first expels all her breath to slenderize herself—then "pulls" in her tummy and lifts her breasts to "hourglass" herself.

Huntresses sometimes ask me, "Should I hire a professional photographer?" No. Pros are great for wedding albums and business annual reports, but not your online picture. If you're itching to pay someone to make you look even more beautiful on the site, engage a local makeup artist and say you want natural-looking "makeup for the camera," which is totally different from what you put on your face for a date.

A client once hired a French makeup artist named Simone to "fix" my face for the cover of one of my audio programs. After an hour of sitting in the chair under bright lights while she futzed with brushes and pencils, pots and goo, I was dying of curiosity. I asked her if I could look in the mirror. Simone shook her head. I thought she was kidding, so I surreptitiously snatched it off the counter. I gasped at the ghoulish face plastered with gobs of makeup staring back at me. Simone pulled the mirror out of my hand, muttering, "Zat ees makeup for zee camera only. It ees completely different." How right she was! It was the best and most natural-looking photo ever taken of me.

Huntresses' Clothes

Hunters are not going to analyze your garb so, unless it's too revealing or too prim, don't worry about it. However, take a tip from an unusual source, the *Journal of Personality and Social Psychology*. Researchers showed men pictures of women wearing clothing in a wide variety of colors. Then the questioning began:

"Sir, tell us which women you would like to kiss."

"Which would you like to have sex with?"

"Which would you be willing to spend a lot of money on?"

In all three cases the winning lady was usually wearing red.[7] Why? This sizzling hot hue physically stimulates a faster heartbeat and heavier breathing. So post your picture as a lady in red, and then check your in-box. If you don't have any red clothes, a red backdrop serves the same purpose.

Huntresses' Background

Unless you're in a jail, a house of ill repute, or surrounded by women more beautiful than you, don't worry about the background. Of these three negative settings, the last is the worst. Male subjects viewing a series of women's photos invariably judged a lady less appealing if the previous female had been more attractive.[8] Ditto if any other woman in the same shot was more alluring. In fact, unless you're with a somewhat beauty challenged acquaintance, leave other women out of your secondary pictures. Why subject yourself to comparisons?

Number of Photos and Poses

Males joke about being a "breast man," "butt man," or "leg man," and you want to cover all of these—shall we say, "special interests." Post one shot tastefully revealing your legs from just smidgeon higher than the knees down. Make the second a modestly covered head to

♀ Chemistry Sparker #14

Photo Tips: Wear Red; Apply Camera-Ready Makeup; and Have a Shot for Each "Special Interest"

Just before the camera clicks, briefly close your eyes to enlarge your pupils. Exhale all your breath and further pull in your tummy. Wear red for your primary photo and, in addition, casual but conservative full-body shots—make sure a leg man, breast man, or butt man can find what he's looking for. Now, with expertly applied camera ready makeup—lots of it to look like none—you'll get some possibly life-changing photographs.

waist shot, torso in profile, and no cleavage. To please the third set of aficionados, have one full body "rear" shot but with your face turned around toward the camera. That plus a couple of face shots and you've got all bases covered.

A Devious Digital Tip for Both Sexes

As you now know, throughout nature a symmetrical insect, fish, bird, reptile, amphibian, invertebrate, or humanoid is considered hotter by other insects, fish, birds, reptiles, amphibians, invertebrates, and humanoids.

Unless you are one of those rare genetically blessed beasts (.001 percent of the population) whose face is utterly symmetrical, turn it ever so slightly away from the camera. That disguises any microscopic imbalance that your Quarry could mistake as you being less than perfectly symmetrical.

Being a believer in truth in advertising, I hesitate to share the following. But with a little computer expertise—and a lot *chutzpah*—you can rival any competing symmetrical creature on the service. Here's how.

Chemistry Sparker #15

Enhance Your Looks with the "Mirror Trick"

Take a full-face picture of you facing directly into the camera. Then make a computer image of one side of your face, flip it over, and put it on the other side. You'll be dumbfounded how fantastic you look with perfect symmetry. Is this cheating? Well, only half!

Your Online Name

If a neuroscientist had been sitting next to Shakespeare at the auditions for *Romeo and Juliet* and heard the lines "What's in a name? That which we call a rose by any other name would smell as sweet," he'd shout, WRONG! And he'd be right. Would a bouquet of flatulence smell as sweet?

The millisecond your name pops up on that dating service screen, your Quarry's hippocampus runs it through its gargantuan memory bank to see if your name has a positive, negative, or somewhat neutral association.

If you think names don't affect attraction, consider this. Hunters, let's say a friend tells you can have a blind date with a Hortense or a Heather. Which would you chose? Ladies, sight unseen, you must pick between a Melvin and a Mark. I'll place my bets on Heather and Mark.

To prove the "what's in a name" concept, researchers posted a sign and a half-dozen girls' pictures on a college bulletin board announcing a supposed upcoming pageant.[9] Written under each picture was a female's false name. The girls were all equally attractive and the students had to vote for one of six contestants for beauty queen. They then repeated the same study at another college with the same pictures but the girls' names were changed under the photos. Here are the results averaged. The girls named Heather got 59 votes, the ones called Jennifer received 52, and Kathy 47. The Gertrudes and Harriets got only 14 votes, and the poor Ethels just 11. That's 159 votes for the girls with the predetermined attractive names and 39 for the others.

Hunters, it seems the ladies are even pickier when it comes to your name. They preferred one-syllable monikers with a hard-stressed front consonant.[10] Names like Curt, Dirk, Grant, Kent, Nash, Pierce, and Troy give females a tiny electrochemical jolt. If you are a Michael, Christopher, Daniel, Joseph, or Ronald, go by Mike, Chris, Dan, Joe, or Ron.

Conversely, gentlemen, if you are thirty-five or older, take the opposite counsel. With age and sophistication a lady prefers a two-syllable name. It sounds classier.

♀♂ Chemistry Sparker #16

Choose a Real, Proven-to-Please Pseudonym

Don't try to be clever or cute with a made-up moniker. Huntresses, select a bona-fide girl's name with as much thought as you'd choose your future daughter's. Your fave is taken? No problem. Just add some underscores or a symbol to it.

Ditto, Hunters. But avoid names like "Manson" or "Bundy." You don't want your Quarry subconsciously connecting it with a serial killer's.

You like her picture? You're impressed by his profile? Now it's time to plan your strategy. But first I must extend my sympathies to the millions of misguided Huntresses who suffer an atavistic ailment spread by word of mouth. They are under the impression that the male of our species must first write the female. Absolutely untrue. Those were the dark ages of computer dating, and it's time for us all to see the light.

Your First Message

Everyone who has ever sent a message to an attractive someone on a dating site has endured the agony of a condition I'm all too familiar with—writer's block. I feel your pain all the more because it's ten times more challenging to write about yourself. After the "Hi," "Hello," "Hey," "Yo," or "How's it going," your fingers freeze. What should I say to this Quarry whose picture and profile I like?

To excavate pearls of wisdom on the subject, I ran an online search about how to present yourself in your first message—and came up with a mere 333 million hits. Most of the suggestions were the same: Be upbeat, check your spelling, demonstrate your sense of humor, mention any shared elements, tell her about your hobbies and interests, tell him about your taste in music, movies, or thirteenth-century madrigals.

Who Is Your Quarry Really Interested In?

Ponder this: Of course your Quarry is curious about you. But who is she more interested in? Right, herself. Who is he most going to enjoy hearing about? Himself, of course. So in your introductory message, write about your Quarry's favorite subject—him or herself. In fact, avoid using the word "I" as much as possible and try to start as many sentences as you can with *you* or *your*. When you sprinkle *you* like salt and pepper throughout your message, your reader finds it an irresistible spice. Gentlemen, applaud her qualities. Ladies, compliment his demeanor. How many people do you think will click "delete" in the middle of reading about themselves?

There's a saying in sales, "When you're tellin', you're not sellin'," and it's true here too. You don't need to sell yourself further because your picture and profile do the basic job. Besides, the most enticing thing about you is what's in your Quarry's imagination and fantasies. That's what keeps computer-dating companies in business.

Talk About What You Read Between the Lines

Even more tantalizing than talking about your Quarry's concrete qualities is what you, and only you, read between the lines about their intangible magnificence. Go through the profile again with a fine-tooth comb and get a sense of the inner person, not the outward physical appearance that any old love seeker ogles. Tell her you sense her creativity, gentleness, kindness, and honesty. Tell him you feel his integrity, dependability, loyalty, or leadership qualities.

This is not just speculation. The *Journal of Social Issues* proved the overwhelmingly greater response to that approach in a study called, "Can You See the Real Me?" about detecting your Quarry's "true self" on the Internet.[11]

Chemistry Sparker #17

Forget the External. Write About Your Quarry's Internal Qualities

Read your Quarry's profile with an "inner" eye. Then tell her about, say, the openness and gentleness that shines through her writing. Comment on his self-assured style that has depth and his humor that came jumping off the screen at you.

Your Quarry will admire your insight and good taste. It confirms what they've known all along—they are special and wonderful. And they want to meet the person who recognizes that.

Before sending, check your message yet again. If you've written something that could be sent to any other woman or man on the site, you're missing the target. Start over.

A Beautiful Tip from an Unsightly Man

Although the next Sparker is for both Hunters and Huntresses, it works better on females. In the play *Cyrano de Bergerac* the beautiful Roxanne fell in love, sight unseen, with a hideous-looking man who, beneath her balcony, described a kiss as "A wish that longs to be confirmed, a rosy circle drawn around the verb 'to love.'"[12]

Every woman has an inner Roxanne. If you're a sucker for a pretty face, she's more of one for a well-turned phrase. Words work wonders and, although you don't want to wax as poetically as Cyrano, take a hint from the verbal heartthrob by spicing up your adjectives. All you need to do is use the thesaurus feature on your computer to impress.

♀ ♂ Chemistry Sparker #18

Create Magic in Your Message with a Thesaurus

Don't use words that are as common as weeds and just as unwelcome. If you want to tell your Quarry that her profile was "interesting," run a synonym search and then substitute a word like, *enchanting, engrossing, or intriguing*.

Huntresses, tell him his profile *mesmerized, impressed or captivated* you. Your less common words and expressions of sentiment demonstrate that you're a cut above the rest of the trite, online love seekers waiting to ride off into the sunset with "the one."

Now let's go from written Sparkers to spoken Sparkers.

CHAPTER 5

How to Spark Chemistry in
Your First Conversation

After the looking and luring—either in person or online—is over, the real road to the bed, beyond, and maybe forever begins at "Hi," "Hello," "How do you do," or "Hey." What follows in the next few seconds determines whether there will even be a next few seconds, minutes, hours, days, weeks, or years. Hunters and Huntresses must use diverse strategies if they want the first conversation to culminate in making a date.

Hunters, as you know, the minute you open your mouth, your Quarry is evaluating your intelligence, character, kindness, creativity, sense of humor, and everything else on her want-in-a-partner list. Huntresses, he is eyeing your attractiveness and how receptive you are to him. Clearly, the first conversation is a bigger challenge for males, so let's start there. However, women, do not skip it! These insights into the male psyche are crucial for you to have a successful hunting expedition.

Chemistry Sparking "Pickup Lines."
(Hunters, Bite Your Tongue!)

My shelf holding books for men on meeting women sags from the weight. Practically all the books include a chapter on clever opening lines, but most would only work on an eighty-year-old nymphomaniac when she was crunked. They are penned by elastic-facts players who brag they could seduce any woman, anytime, anywhere. Gentlemen, you'd have better luck finding the Loch Ness monster than a one-size-fits-all opening line.

Evidence aside, the question of "What is a good one" is such a pathetic perennial, an invasive weed that won't die, that I must address it here:

A group of sociologists who wanted their names forever enshrined in professional journals eavesdropped on male opening gambits in bars, restaurants, parties, laundromats, and other incubators of "intergender acquaintanceship," as they called them.[1] The analysts divided the overheard lines into three categories: the *direct,* the *innocuous,* and the *cute flippant.* Here are the stats on which approaches scored with the ladies and which hit the skids.

Women found the third category of opening lines, "cute flippant," abominable. The second category, "innocuous" (a casual pleasantry to elicit conversation), came in second. The most successful was the "direct" approach, with no pretense of the pickup being anything else. Researchers wrote, "The approaches which rated the highest were direct approaches displaying positive character traits as well as cultural knowledge."[2] The conversation opener was even more welcome when the Hunter, with a confident demeanor, voiced a word of embarrassment.

If you're still not comfortable with that, here is the world's second-best approach. According to the "Leil Lowndes Unofficial Survey of

Women Sixteen to Sixty," women preferred it nine times out of ten, and it has stood the test of time. I prefer it. My mother preferred it. And her mother before her preferred it. The trumpet blare please: "Hello, my name is _____. And yours?" Try it. She'll like it.

Unless a beautiful woman sounds like she's hog calling, you won't take special note of her voice, but she will yours. It can be beautiful music or microphone feedback to her. Mother Nature programs females to respond viscerally to a deep male voice because it signals more testosterone, which, in turn, makes your sperm stronger, which, in turn, makes you a better begetter of babies.[3]

♂ Chemistry Sparker #19

Forget Macho. Use a Slightly Self-Effacing Direct Approach

Approach your Quarry with total confidence—but verbalize a slight touch of self-effacement. Example: "Hi, I feel a little embarrassed about this, but I'd really like to meet you. My name is . . . " Presenting yourself that way displays self-assurance, intelligence, and no pretense. You don't believe it works? Check out the original study called, quite aptly, "Preference for Opening Lines" in the references.

What Every Woman Needs to Know—But Few Do

The word "rejection" mainlines terror into the veins of the most confident of men.[4] They can hardly say the "R word." Guys wrack their brains for pick-up lines, read books on how to be a "player," take online courses, and practice personality tricks to make you swoon. Some spend thousands to attend seminars. I've spoken at these conferences and am shocked how it petrifies a guy that you won't accept his overture. He has nightmares of someone shouting out, "Hey, everybody, look at that sniveling little critter. He actually thinks he can pick up the likes of her." The crowd laughs uproariously, and stripped of his manhood, he crawls away.

Guys Just Don't Get It!

Girl, you must make your interest outrageously blatant. One of the country's most respected sex and relationship researchers determined that 97 percent of men just don't "get it" when you signal them.[5] It's not his fault. Never forget: The male brain is not constructed to sense subtleties in nonverbal communication.

Some years ago, before my cousin, Rory, married his lovely wife, Camilla, he was visiting me. A nearby pub is known as one of the best meat markets in New York City, so off we went. I noticed a beautiful redhead sitting at the bar who kept smiling at Rory. To me and every other woman in the room, it was as obvious as a fly in a sugar bowl. Rory talked to a few girls and, not finding anyone special, suggested we leave. Walking home, I commented, "Gee Rory, it's really too bad you didn't see any girls you liked."

"Oh, I did," he said.

"Really, which ones?"

"Did you happen to notice the girl at the end of the bar with the long red hair?"

"Yes!" I sputtered. "The one who was giving you the clear come-on signals."

"Giving me the what?" he gasped.

"The poor girl kept flirting her little red head off trying to get your attention."

"C'mon Leil, don't tease me like that."

"Rory, I'm serious. Her signals were as clear as crystal to me and every other woman in the bar. And obviously clear as mud to you."

To this day, he thinks I was kidding.

The Case for Female Proceptivity

For female what? The word *proceptive* is sociological/anthropological lingo for the female initiating the relationship. In order to produce successful products, a company requires both quantity and quality. On Planet Earth, males are responsible for quantity of output and females are in charge of quality. It's true all throughout nature. Female mammals in Mother Nature's magnificent skies, seas, and earth are extremely picky about their "sperm donors." A ladybug, bee, bird, or fish spots her preferred target bug, bee, bird, or fish. Then, by tongue flicking, self-licking, or obscene sucking sounds, she lures her chosen Quarry. Chuckling inside, if animals could chuckle, she pretends to run away. He chases her, convinced that all those spicy signals mean sure sex.

Ladies, learn from the lower creatures. They are smarter than you in this sense because they openly practice female proceptivity. Your mantra should be "If you want a top-rate mate, you must initiate." Females are the logical pursuers. Society, however, has repressed our natural proclivities. Just as many gays and lesbians once felt obligated to hide theirs, it's time for us all to come out of the closet!

Huntresses' Pickup Lines (Try a Few, He'll Love It!)

Ladies, I'm not even going to bother with the kid stuff suggestions. You'll get the same old chestnuts about being the first to make eye contact and to smile from plenty of other sources. And, yes, it's good advice. To obliterate any lingering doubt about its overwhelming power, the research project, "Giving Men the Come-on: Effect of Eye Contact and Smiling in a Bar Environment" proves it.[6] It's elementary. It's effortless. And yes, it works to lure him over. But we're not just talking "lure" in this book; we're talking about creating that chemical Spark.

Girl, I cautioned Hunters to forget they ever heard the words "pickup line." Conversely, I implore you to learn a few. When the bars/restaurants/parties/laundromats study was reversed, males responded overwhelmingly to women's opening lines. "Reactions to Heterosexual Opening Gambits" proved that the direct, innocuous— and even cute-flippant ones—were equally effective when coming from a female.[7]

You'd want to wear a bag over your head while delivering any of the following pickup lines, and I am *not* suggesting any of them verbatim. I present them merely to give you an idea of the corny phrases proven to produce the desired results. Here were the researchers' scripted lines for the ladies:

- They directed some women to approach men with a smile and say, "When I first saw you, I thought about introducing you to my girlfriend, but I'm not that generous."
- Others followed their Quarry with a pen in their hands and asked, "Did you drop this?" They then laughed and confessed. "That was a pretty lamebrain excuse for me to talk to you, wasn't it?"

- A third group said, "Can I say I met a hot guy tonight, or do I have to lie to my diary?"

Do these lines sound cheesy? Yes. Corny? Yes. Dumb? Yes. *Déclassé*? Yes. Do they work? A resounding *yes!* I hear you thinking, "Oh, I couldn't do that!" But consider this: If you don't awaken his napping neurons with something shocking, you may never meet him. Which is worse?

♀ Chemistry Sparker #20

Huntresses, Plan Some Opening Lines!

Sisters, think like a guy and plan phrases to meet your next Potential Love Partner, whom we'll call your PLP. There is no need to be quite as outrageous as the ladies in the study were directed, but write your own opening lines. Be creative and courageous. Raise the bar on your comfort level, and be a *little* outrageous.

But Won't He Think I'm Being Aggressive?

The short answer is no. Here is the longer one: It's not just the senile, the sleepless, and alcoholics who suffer memory loss. The male ego has an uncanny ability to rewrite history and conveniently disremember who approached whom. Remember, his prefrontal cortex is not the best egg in his basket when saturated with dopamine and testosterone. For the rest of your future life together, he will brag to your mutual friends that he, the successful Hunter, made the first move. Why? Because, as I said before, thanks to the male's more sluggish gray-matter transmissions, his "instant" is slower. When your blatant come-on finally dawns on him, it could be the first moment he thinks he's noticed you.

At a neighborhood gathering I ran into a friend, Melissa Richards, who had been married to her husband, Randy, for twelve years. I asked her how they'd met. "Leil, I shamelessly stalked him," she laughed, and then revealed the details. When they were students at Stanford, Melissa spotted him studying at another table in the library. She instantly felt the Spark and kept sneaking peeks at Randy. When he noticed, she smiled. He returned the smile perfunctorily but went back to looking at his books. This scenario repeated itself the next day. Obviously Randy didn't feel the Spark for Melissa.

On evening three, Melissa decided to take action. She hid behind one of the shelves in the library at the usual time Randy came to study. Pretending to just enter, she came over to him and lied that she'd been sitting at that table earlier in the afternoon and had lost a contact lens. Randy crawled around the floor helping her look for it. But to no avail, of course, because Melissa never wore contacts. He then went back to his books.

Almost ready to give up, she decided to try one more ploy. She got a cup of coffee at the campus café, sat at his table, and started sipping it while studying. She reached for another book and—oops—the coffee just happened to spill. Randy, the perfect gentleman, raced into the men's room for towels to swab it up. When he finished she touched his arm and jokingly purred, "Oh, you are my hero."

For the first time, it seemed, Randy looked her directly in the eyes. It was Melissa's physical touch that lit the Spark. "Uh, let me get you another coffee," he stammered.

"Oh, thanks. I'll join you." Melissa replied. They walked side by side into the café. If it had been a movie, the music would crescendo as "The End" comes up on the big screen.

Several weeks after the neighborhood get-together they invited me to dinner, and this time I thought it would be fun to ask Randy how they met. Here's his story:

"It was at the university library, and the first time I saw Melissa I knew she was the woman for me. I didn't even know if she drank coffee, but I'm glad she did because I asked her if she'd like one with me. And the rest," he grinned, "is history." Melissa smiled demurely at him and kicked me under the table.

So sisters, secretly revel in your prowess and smile shamelessly into the eyes of your new Quarry. Go after him with barefaced abandon. He'll never remember how it happened.

If, despite all the evidence to the contrary, you still hesitate to deliver "a line," there is the substitute testosterone tweaker that Melissa used—the power of touch.

♀ Chemistry Sparker #21

Trick Him into Touching You

Find an excuse for bodily contact—any excuse! For example, wear a bracelet or necklace and, upon spotting your Quarry, surreptitiously click open the clasp. Then ask him, "Oops, excuse me. Could I trouble you to help me put it back on?" Another ploy is to ask him what time it is. When he tells you, pretend to be surprised and jokingly grab his arm to see his watch, as though you need proof that he's telling the truth.

Even the most innocent physical contact gets his hormones hopping, *especially* if he's rescuing a fair lady from a distressing situation.

The Physical Side of "Hello"

Huntresses, you're in luck if you've met your Quarry in a somewhat professional setting because you can employ the power of bodily touch naturally. It's called shaking hands. People think, "I can't read your mind," but cognitive science might take issue with that. Your thoughts produce physiological responses that are manifested in your autonomic, or involuntary, nervous system. Your every thought has a subtle influence on your heart rate, blood pressure, respiratory rate, and sweat glands. Lie detectors are built on that basis, and science has succeeded in implanting a device in the brain, enabling quadriplegics to control robots with just their thoughts.[8]

You can secretly employ that cognitive power. While holding his hand, transmit a subliminal message by lightly placing your pointing finger on his pulse. In a sense, it is touching his heart, because his pulse is a wave traveling directly from the heart. Then press your whole hand against his so tightly that you couldn't shove a marble between your palms. After pumping the traditional few seconds, when he starts to pull his hand away, squeeze it and pull it slightly closer to you. Then harness the power of your mind to Spark him.

♀ Chemistry Sparker #22

Think Hot Thoughts While Shaking His Hand

While holding his hand, gaze into his eyes and silently say, "You are really hot and I want to have sex with you." Your soundless monologue—some would call it "dirty thoughts"—camouflaged by your professional demeanor, gives your face just the right expression to ignite a tiny Spark. To a certain extent, mind reading is possible—especially if your mind is saying something he wants to hear.

Ladies, all of the above little Sparkers have a cumulative effect. He'll never guess that what he felt was due to your protracted handshake, pressing his pulse, silent salacious messaging, or surprise touch. He'll just tell your friends, "I felt an instant Spark when I met her."

Spark Your Quarry During the First Conversation

Gentlemen, as you now know, the topic you discuss is way less crucial than what the casual chat reveals about you. Gentlemen age fifty-plus, you may remember the old eight-track music tapes in the 1970s. Your Quarry's brain is capable of listening to all tracks simultaneously. Track one: your appearance. Track two: how you move. Track three: your clothes. Track four: your voice. Track five: your intelligence. Track six: your socioeconomic level. Track seven: your personality. And track eight: how you treat her. Remember, her mind isn't one-track like most guys'.

The Rapid Transit System Called the Female Brain

Here is an only slightly exaggerated peek at the simultaneous tracks in the female brain. Let's say you're casually chatting with her about your health club. She's musing, *Great, he's a healthy guy.* But if you mention the gym again later in the conversation, it's, *He's a health freak.* Mention your church. *Nice. He has integrity.* Talk about your place of worship again, and it's, *This guy's a religious fanatic.* You tell her something nice about a buddy. *Good, he has male friends.* But bring up the same buddy later in the conversation? *Maybe he's gay.*

Science buffs, you know a strip of blue litmus paper dunked in a vat of acid turns pink. And if you dip the tip in a single drop of acid on a glass slide, it turns just as pink. Well, the lady's mind is like litmus paper and can't help but make inferences from every drop of your conversation.

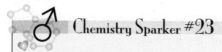

Chemistry Sparker #23

Don't Get Labeled by Repetition or Excessive Emphasis

Hunters, be as careful as a hemophiliac in a razor blade factory during the first conversation. Beware of talking too much about the same thing, and don't return to a previous point unless really relevant. You don't need an undeserved "fanatic" label slapped on your forehead.

She Reads Between the Lines— So Talk Between the Lines

Your goal in this first conversation is to show that you are boyfriend, maybe even husband material. If the woman is really gorgeous, Hunters, you might overlook a little thing like her prison record. Women don't. She secretly dons a Sherlock Holmes cap, packs a magnifying glass in her purse, and slinks stealthily through everything you say for clues to your character.

"But how can I show my good qualities without bragging?" you ask. Here are a few ideas. Her silent reactions are in italics.

- Ask her favorite restaurants. Then drop the names of some of yours—first-class ones, of course. Between the lines she's reading, *He's got good taste.*
- Compliment something she's wearing, say, her bracelet. Ask where she bought it because you want to buy your little sis-

ter a present. *How nice, he's good to his family.* But, darn, you couldn't find anything in the Tiffany's catalogue. *Maybe he's rich.*

- Whatever subject she brings up, say "Tell me more." *He's interested in my mind, not just my body.*

- If at all relevant to the subject, quote something that you read about in the *Wall Street Journal.* If she's more the literary type, try the *New York Review of Books.* It will also impress her if you quote one of your favorite books. (But not this one!)

- If you know anyone in her field, be sure to say, "You should meet . . ." Now you get an A-plus for wanting to further her personal growth.

Chemistry Sparker #24

Talk Between the Lines, Saying, "I Am Husband Material"

It makes sense that, if she's listening between the lines, you should talk between the lines. Never plan an "opening line," but do stockpile ways to allude to your good-guy characteristics. Be subtle, however, very subtle! Don't worry—her x-ray antennae will pick up on them.

A Pivotal Question

As sure as a goose goes barefoot, your Quarry will soon ask, "So what do you do?" It is not necessarily *what* your job is but *how you respond* that could be the life or death sentence on your potential relationship. Prepare an answer that impresses her without seeming to.

From what you now know about how Big Mama programmed the lovely, you might assume her query is solely for determining how much you make. In another era your assumption might be right. But for the most evolutionarily developed women, your vocation signifies something more important than money. It is a key to your character. For a growing number of twenty-first-century women, it doesn't matter whether you are a bigwig who owns half of the entire computer industry or work in the mailroom at Macy's. Women prefer a man of character who can get what he wants in life. If you are CEO of a global firm but despise your profession, you come off as a loser. Conversely, even if you cut cadavers or breed slugs for a living, you're a winner if you like your job because you've achieved what you want.

When she asks, "What do you do?" here is the perfect answer:

♂ Chemistry Sparker #25

Give a Playful but Passionate Answer About Your Work

When she asks what you do, respond with a playful smile and these precise words: "For pleasure or work?" Follow that with, "I'm just kidding, I love my job." Then enthusiastically tell her more.

Sentence number one displays your sense of humor. Sentence two shows you are a positive person. Sentence three says you are winner because you're not stuck doing a job you don't like.

A note for Huntresses: I know I may be asking the impossible, but if you refrain from asking, "What do you do?" it demonstrates that you are different from nearly every other female on the planet. I know it's not easy, girl, but give it a shot.

Gentlemen, the following conversation tip is gleaned from a study in which men were directed to "confess" a little fault to a new Quarry, something like you always forget your keys or where you parked the car.[9] Because a woman is so used to a Hunter trying to impress her, she finds it charming when you do the opposite.

Chemistry Sparker #26

Make a Tiny Personal Confession

To increase the Chemistry between you, confess a little fault.[10] She'll find your revelatory repartee rare, honest, and endearing. But keep it small. She doesn't want to hear about your bankruptcy declaration, bigamy charge, or bitter divorce.

Today the Who-Impresses-Whom Rules Are Reversed

Beware of trying to impress your Quarry overtly, especially in the money department. There's a good chance she has more money than you anyway. In fact, single women today earn more than single men.[11] Put your effort into showing how much she impresses you. Here's a Sparker that shows you're interested in her job.

Continue asking your Quarry questions about herself and adjust your antennae to tune in to her self-image. Is she proud of being extremely bright? Spiritual? What about an extensive knowledge in a particular field? "How fascinating," you exclaim, "that you've read the twelfth-century *Dialogues de Scaccario* in the original Latin. I'd like to hear more. When would you be free for dinner with me so you can tell me all about it?"

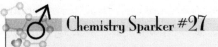

Chemistry Sparker #27

Be Fascinated by Her Business Card and Ask Questions

When she hands you her business card, don't just peek at it and shove it in your back pocket. Hold it with two hands and gaze at respectfully. Glance at it several times while she tells you about her job. Occasionally nod admiringly and ask more questions about her job.

Here's another question that is perfect for showing nonsexual interest. Ask her, "What is your average day like?"

Chemistry Sparker #28

Show Growing Interest in Her Mind

Men who express their interest gradually are more successful with attractive women than those who show they are immediately impressed.[12] Convince your Quarry you are far more interested in what's between her ears than what is between her thighs. Otherwise, she figures it's just her looks, and you become as important to her as a screen door on a submarine.

Huntress, Are You One in a Million, or One Among a Million?

Huntresses, if you're a gorgeous ten, little short of picking your nose, putting him down, or—for some—lighting a cigarette will turn him off sexually, so your first words are not as crucial. However, males have a derogatory term for women who use lascivious lures and "don't deliver" (hint: initials "C. T."). It's only fair to lay the groundwork during the first conversation that you are not going to hop into bed with him immediately. After you've lured him with sexual signals it's time to show him that you are serious-relationship material. You are one in a million, not one among a million.

Begin the Bait and Switch

Did I just use that awful phrase? Shame on me. But I'm a great believer in "the end justifies the means" as long as it's best for both parties, is not illegal, and doesn't hurt anyone. Your "bait" was tweaking his testosterone in anticipation of hot times to come with you. Your "switch" is flashing something more important—your superior qualities. In the back of his mind (albeit way back at first) are the characteristics he wants in a future wife, like intelligence, compassion, integrity, and fidelity.[13]

There are lots of ways to hint at these. You could bring up a current news story—not one in which celebrities are sleeping together but perhaps something international (intelligence). If it's about a subjugated population, express your dismay (compassion). Tell him how much you respect a friend's honesty (integrity). If the subject of past relationships comes up, make sure you never hint at any extracurricular activities (fidelity).

♀ Chemistry Sparker #29

Reveal Your Substantial Qualities Early in the Conversation

As soon as your sexy lure is successful, start showing the characteristics that quality Quarry considers long-term potential must-haves. Let nothing slip that could destroy that image. Make a conscious effort to plant the seeds that signal, "I am a special woman of superior quality."

Huntresses, this does not mean telling him *too* much about yourself, however. If you read the previous advice for males, telling them to reveal a few tidbits of personal information to his Quarry in the first conversation, ignore it. It doesn't work the other way around. Instead, make your male Quarry wait for a date or two to discover more about you. Keep personal, psychologically revealing stuff to a minimum.[14]

♀ Chemistry Sparker #30

Stick to a Nondisclosure Policy

No matter how much you're sure you're destined to be together, do not make the mistake of spilling your life story. (At this point he's not interested anyway.) Also, try to use the words "I feel" or "I felt" as few times as possible. Unlike you, at first a male is not fascinated by your feelings about anything—except him.

Double Name Talk

Creating Chemistry, as you now know, means inciting neurons in your Quarry's brain to zap messages in all directions like a spreading wildfire. A recent National Institute of Health study showed excitation in several brain regions when hearing one's own name.[15] Here's a way to double them to ignite the flicker into a little Spark.

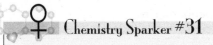

Chemistry Sparker #31

Nudge Your Quarry's Neurons with a Double Name Whammy

Just saying his name is old hat. Double that power. Somewhere, further into the conversation, say your Quarry's first *and* last name to give it a twofold punch. "Palmer Smith, you are so funny." Or his first name twice in response to something he said: "Oh, Palmer, Palmer."

So Far, So Good

Hunters, 1) you've met the lady respectfully, 2) shown husband-material qualities, 3) made a charming tiny personal confession, and 4) proved that she fascinates you as a person.

Huntresses, you 1) either lured him with sex or picked him up, 2) were upbeat, 3) a bit of a mystery woman, and, finally, 4) began the bait and switch by showing wife-worthy substantial qualities.

One or both of you decide it's time for a date.

CHAPTER 6

How to Spark Chemistry on Dates

Dating is the best of times and the worst of times. You feel like you are dancing on the clouds. Then he does something that hurts you to the core. She says something that means you might lose her. You are crushed, and serotonin drops like a cannonball in the lake. Confusion and chaos result.

How heartbreaking that dating has become a competitive sport—or that it is any type of game at all. In an ideal world potential partners would see each other, smile, feel confident, and form a relationship without all the difficulty and drama. But from the instant human animals sniff potential romance, electrical signals in their brains start zapping around like pinballs and their heads spin. Moments later, it's "Tally ho, let the games begin!"

Even if you try to avoid them, as most of us do, sooner or later you and your Quarry find yourselves guessing about each other's motives, gathering evidence, envisioning, estimating, considering, and finally deciding whether to stay together or split. If that doesn't involve difficulty and drama, I don't know what does! Meanwhile,

Mother Nature is loving it. She's kicking you both in your privates, encouraging your anxiety because that makes you crave your Quarry all the more.

But back to the game's starting line. Whether you become hungrier for her or you feel you've had enough of him often happens on the first date. But first you've got to get that date. Here are some ways to ensure success.

Hunters, "Sell" Her on the Date Like a Pro

Whatever else you think about a used car salesmen, he's no dummy in one respect. After his pitch and carefully planned close, he sticks a pen between the prospect's thumb and forefinger—point facing down—and he deftly slides the contract under the tip of the pen. Instead of questioning, "Well, do you want to buy it or not?" he asks the prospect, "When do you want delivery?" They call it the "assumptive close." He takes for granted that of course the customer wants his product.

Take a tip from the pitchman and do the same. The tired old "How about Saturday night?" riff could spell quick rejection. Don't ask your Quarry, *if* she'd like to have dinner with you. Take it as a foregone conclusion that of course she would and just ask *when*.

Try this: "I want to check out the new El Romantico Restaurant. What night would you be free to come with me?" That shows confidence. Worded this way, unless she's thinking, "You dish pit, I would never sit across a table from you," she's at a loss for what to say. She can't tell you she's given up eating or booked up for the rest of her life, so her only refusal resort is a revelatory humming or hawing. Then at least you know the score and won't put yourself out on a limb for another rejection later.

Another twist is what sales professionals call the "alternative close." The salesman once again "assumes" his prospect wants the car and asks, "Will you be taking the black one or the green one?" Here's how to employ that tactic. Tell your date you'd like to take her to either El Romantico or L'Eleganti Restaurant. Which would she prefer?

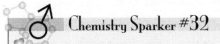

Chemistry Sparker #32

Use the "Assumptive" or "Alternative" Close

When offering your Quarry the pleasure of spending a few hours with you, expand the window of opportunity. Simply ask, "when?" as though you're sure there's not a snowball's chance in a sauna that she'd say no. Another ploy is to ask her which of two places she'd prefer.

Crack the Old Hard-to-Get Chestnut

Huntresses, you are talking to Mr. Magnificent Specimen and your white matter is making so many connections to every word that passes his lips that you can hardly concentrate on the order of them. But finally you hear the sequence you've been salivating for, "Would you like to go . . . "

You suppress shouting a jubilant "Yes!" before he finishes the sentence. Let's say he invites you to an excellent film you've been meaning to see. What should you do? Choose one.

1. Look like you're pondering the question.
2. Tell him that you're terribly sorry, but you're tied up that evening but perhaps another time.

3. Give him a big smile and tell him you'd love to see that film.

Answer: None of the above! Instead, act pleased and exclaim, "[his name], I'd love to go out with YOU!" This lets your Quarry know your interest lies in spending time with *him*, not in whatever he's suggesting.

♀ Chemistry Sparker #33

Don't Say Yes to the Date. Say Yes to *Him*

Let your Quarry know it's not the activity you're interested in, it's the man. Your surprise answer gives him an immediate pleasure Spark. Whatever activity he suggests, here are your scripted words. Say his name and add, "I'd love to go out with *you.*"

"But," you may be wondering, "what happens if he doesn't ask me out?" Not to worry. Read on.

How to Get the Date without Asking

Reluctantly, you must admit that there is the rare possibility that asking you out didn't even cross his mind. The following tactic is rapidly gaining bigender and generational respect everywhere.

Simply deliver a big smile and one of the following:

"Trevor, we should get together some evening."

"Patrick, let's go party one night."

"Lance, I'd love to go out with you sometime."

This one, followed by a wink, is my favorite: "The next time you feel like asking somebody for a date, think of me."

Now, that's female proceptivity at its finest!

♀ Chemistry Sparker #34

Say "Yes" Before He Asks

If he's lily-livered about asking you for a date, a broad hint gives him the guts to ask. If he's dense, it plants the seeds. And if he didn't think to ask you out (foolish man!), you do the job for him. This way you haven't actually popped the question, but you've made it obvious that his invitation will definitely not be met with his greatest fear, rejection.

The Most Chemistry-Sparking First Date

The constant quandary: Where should we go on our first date? Hunters, what would you most enjoy? A football game? A skating rink? An action movie? Fast action gives guys a dopamine rush.

Huntresses, what about you? A French restaurant? An Italian restaurant? A Chinese restaurant? Fine cuisine and bonding conversation give females a dopamine and oxytocin rush.

Hmm, what he'd like to do (an exciting activity) and what she'd like to do (relaxed dining) are very different destinations. The solution? The best first date is both: an activity followed by dinner.

The First Half of the Date

Start the evening off with something exciting. A thriller movie, a strenuous physical activity, or maybe even something a little scary. The study "Evidence for Heightened Sexual Attraction Under Conditions of High Anxiety" proved a strong link between love and fear.[1] Lovers and wannabe lovers on screen, on stage, and in novels face frightening forces together. Prehistoric beasts, ruthless killers, intergalactic invaders, and a passel of other evil forces threaten to tear the couple asunder. Did it ever cross your mind that the lovers might not even be turned on by each other if it weren't for the immense adversity they had to tackle together? Shakespeare knew its power. What would be the big thrill for Romeo and Juliet if the Montagues didn't want to kill the Capulets?[2]

A stimulating activity Sparks the dopamine thrill, resulting in a phenomenon called "excitation transfer" or "transference effect," in which your brain assumes the thrill came from being with that particular person, not necessarily the activity.[3] A form of psychotherapy called neurolinguistic programming (NLP) calls this effect "anchoring."[4] When you feel excitement on a date, even though it's due to an outside force, you connect or "anchor" it to your Quarry. Just seeing her face again can bring on the exciting stimulation you felt. Hearing his voice reinvokes the neuronal animation you experienced on the first date.

♀♂ Chemistry Sparker #35

Date Part One: Do Something Stirring

Do something that generates electrochemical activity in your Quarry's brain as the first part of the date. Perhaps a physical activity or sports events for Hunters or an emotionally stirring experience like a concert or heart-wrenching film for Huntresses. Whatever either of you feels on this first date will rub off on the other through excitation transfer.

The Second Half of the Date

Hunters, you may have the best of intentions and think you're being gracious by asking your date where she'd like to dine. But you should choose. Otherwise you might come across as unknowledgeable or indecisive. Make a reservation and confirm it a few hours beforehand. You look bad if your table isn't ready just because some dude named Brad Pitt made a last-minute reservation.

The eatery need not be pricey, but it should reflect your personality. Do you want your Quarry to think of you as artistic? Take her to a restaurant where artists go. Want to come off as a successful businessman? Take her to a restaurant where successful businesspeople go. You want her to see you as a cool dude? Take her to a restaurant where cool dudes go. There is one exception. You'd like her to think you're a jock? Do *not* take her to a sports bar—unless that's where she's dying to go. In that case, she's pretty special and you might consider proposing on the spot.

Huntresses, if he is charmingly naive enough to let you choose the dining venue, don't make the same mistake that Phil's date, Goldilocks, did in Chapter 2. Unless you're positive he's a high roller, play lowball. Choose a charming little eatery within his budget.

A place with a nice ambiance and low lighting is a plus because both of you will seem more attractive.

In one study, "Effects of Aesthetic Surroundings," people were shown pictures of opposite sex individuals in various venues, some superior, some shoddy. Researchers then asked, "Pick out the best-looking people." The folks in rooms with beautiful chandeliers, grand pianos, fine art, and other opulent etceteras were almost invariably chosen over those in greasy spoons.[5] Of course, the photos were of the same people in both settings.

♀♂ Chemistry Sparker #36

Date Part Two: Do Something Relaxing (Preferably with Food)

After the emotionally or physically electrically charged activity, wind down the date with a quiet little dinner where you can chat and enhance the bonding Chemistry between you. This two-part date sequence should leave no uncomfortable silences because, of course, you'll discuss how much you both loved the activity.

Eating Sparkers

Hunters, as a real guy-type guy, you probably equate etiquette with extending a pinkie when drinking from a cup and wonder why your Quarry cares about manners. It's because Mother Nature reminds the lovely that no man who picks his teeth with the edge of a sugar packet is going to be promoted to the top. When gravy dribbles from your open mouth, her dopamine level dips down like a thermometer dropped in the snow.

Huntresses, you can make it a more exciting dining experience for him by a few gentle, subtle, but not too suggestive moves like sliding your glass up next to his or running your fingers seductively up and down the stem of your wine glass. Let his fantasies do the rest.

On this and the many subsequent dates, you are both contemplating whether you want to continue with this PLP (Potential Love Partner) or call it quits. Where you go and what you talk about on each date factors into whether there will be a next. Here are dating Sparkers to use on every date right on up to the altar or moving-in together day.

Play Games with Your Quarry

Now we're talking different type of games—sports, hobbies, interests. I'm sure you've heard that females bond by talking and males by doing things together. It's not a myth.

Huntresses, think back to the early days of your relationship. Were you moved when you discovered he felt deeply about something you believed in? Perhaps it increased your sense of closeness to him when you learned of his shared passion for animal rights, respect for the elderly, or concern for the environment. Likewise, a Hunter's bonding sentiments bubble up when you tell him you too enjoy bowling, bungee jumping, watching boxing matches, or whatever his passion.

Girl, if you truly do enjoy his sport, highlight the heck out of it and suggest you do it a lot. Just make sure you truly do like it or else you could sentence yourself to years in noisy bowling alleys, sweaty gyms, or on the wrong end of a scary elastic rope. My regular readers know I usually subscribe to the "fake it 'til you make it" philosophy of life. But when it comes to serious relationships, swear off pretending. Otherwise, when your ruse is revealed, it's over. The axiom here is "Fake it and you'll break it."

Bethany, a good friend of mine since high school, met the man she wanted to set sail with on the Love Boat, but it sank because of her lie. One time I had talked Bethany into coming on a scuba dive with me. She did, but later, while tearing off her tank, told me she'd hated it. But she certainly didn't hate what happened at the beach bar afterward. Don, a fellow diver sitting with us, introduced us to his buddy, Baird. "A big-time diver," as Don described him.

Baird asked, "How did you enjoy the dive, girls?"

Bethany squealed and, smiling as wide a crescent moon, lied, "Oh, I just loved it! I can't wait to do it again!" Right on her clever cue, Baird asked her to join him for a dive the following week. She did, and the following week, and the following week—and the following week. Baird adored the fact that she was becoming such an avid new diver. They started dating regularly.

Bethany was so busy with Baird that I didn't get a chance to see her very often. The next time I heard from her was six months later. She was in tears.

"What happened, Beth?" Between sobs, she told me the story. It seemed Baird wanted to go diving every weekend. All he'd talk about at dinner was their last dive and his plans for the next. From what I could determine, Bethany's ruse about her passion for diving became a drag. Her laughter at Baird's diving jokes sounded less sincere. Her smile froze as she listened to his stories of great dives.

Finally, one Thursday evening, Bethany told Baird that she wasn't going diving with him that weekend because she hadn't had her hair done in months and she needed a facial due to all the wind and sand. The next weekend she found another excuse.

Bethany didn't hear from him one week, and when she called, he said he'd begun diving with some other friends and had met someone new, "a dedicated diver," he told her. She didn't have to finish the story. Baird loved diving and he also loved women. He wanted both, and Bethany only filled half that bill.

Activities that you enjoy shoot dopamine levels up just like the chemical rush you felt on your first dates. If you truly love the activity, you continue to "transfer" those euphoric feelings to your PLP. If you quit, the dopamine quits along with it.

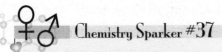

Chemistry Sparker #37

Play the Same Games

If there is an activity that your Potential Love Partner enjoys that you like too, play it up big time. Although it's true for both of you, joint activity is a higher priority for Hunters. It's a guy's way of bonding and bringing you closer. But be real—or be wretched.

Chemistry-Sparking Conversation on Every Date

As a shy teen, just talking with someone of the male gender made my heart beat like a repeater pistol and my face look like a sunburned lobster. Before a date I'd torture myself trying to think of topics to discuss that would make him like me more. I wish I'd known the following.

He Says/She Says, What?

The gender-preferred topics are pretty common knowledge these days. If you missed some of the popular books on the subject, here are the crib notes.

- Huntresses tend to talk about people. Men concentrate on things.
- Huntresses speculate on feelings. Hunters stick to facts.
- Huntresses fancy the abstract. Hunters favor the concrete.
- Huntresses share emotions. Hunters prefer the logical.
- Huntresses conjecture harmony with colleagues. Hunters consider competition and who's on top.

Once again, like everything we're talking about in this book, it all makes exquisite evolutionary sense. "Fight or flight" has been an instinctive male reaction ever since his gorilla ancestor strutted down Noah's gangplank. Once on dry land he had to fight for dominance over the other simians, which gives insight into a Hunter's conversation preferences. He likes to talk of his dominance over today's human baboons—his achievements, adventures, concepts, politics, objects, and big toys.

The neurological female equivalent to "fight or flight" is "tend and befriend."[6] It's the instinctive female response ever since her gorilla ancestress followed him down the gangplank. Once on dry land, tending to her tiny ones and keeping them safe was a full-time job. That gives insight into a Huntress's conversational preferences. She enjoys exploring relationships, feelings, intuition, and perceptions of other people.

Oh, did I forget to mention that men like to talk about sports? Girl, it's great if you can too. But be careful. Clashing with him on the MLB's top pitching rotation last year could strike you out in the first inning of your relationship.

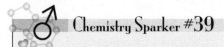

Chemistry Sparker #38

Speak in Your Quarry's Gender

Huntresses, catch yourself if you find yourself talking too much about people and your feelings. Ditto, Hunters, if you start expounding excessively on facts and competitive situations. In short: Huntresses, stick more to things, facts, and the concrete. Hunters, try exploring abstracts and both your feelings.

Hunters, Follow Your Quarry's Rhythm

Even if you had the above crib sheet on your lap, having great conversations on dates can be tough because you don't *think* like the other sex. But you can learn to speak in the other's style. Here are a few hints.

Hunters, you may have noticed that females have a different conversational rhythm. After stating an opinion, they often throw the conversation back with a tag line like, "What about you?" or "What do you think?"

Chemistry Sparker #39

Play Conversational Volleyball

Gentlemen, after you've stated an opinion, ask hers. Once she picks her dropped jaw up off the table, she'll adore answering—and you for asking. Make sure she is talking at least half the time, maybe more. As long as *she's* talking, she'll think *you're* a fascinating conversationalist.

Don't let there be too many long silences. Those make females uncomfortable and fear you're not communicating.

Huntresses, Don't Fill in the Blanks

Huntresses, this may come as a surprise, but men don't need—or even want—to be communicating every minute the two of you are together. The male mind is quite comfortable with compatible silence.[7] The lack of talking is not because he doesn't feel close to you. It is not because he has nothing to say. It's just that many smart men don't feel they need to fill up the air with words.[8]

As we've discussed, your Quarry's neurotransmissions don't zap from one thing to the next as quickly. After you've said something, a male likes time to digest it and collect his thoughts before speaking. If you jump in trying to cover the uncomfortable (to you) silence, it could be jarring and destroy the closeness he's feeling during your mutual quiet time.

♀ Chemistry Sparker #40

Don't Feel Obligated to Fill the Silences

When a lull comes in the conversation, simply enjoy it with him. A self-assured man is not the least bit uncomfortable with compatible silence. In fact, he'll appreciate it because you're probably his first date who doesn't talk just to make conversation.

Give a "You Fit My LoveMap" Feeling

You can take a big step toward enhancing your relationship with a simple verbal tweak. Every word and tone has an emotional impact. Hearing a familiar or unfamiliar song creates a very different neurochemical reaction. A dancer named Svetlana whom I met at a neuroscience lecture told me about a brain scan she had volunteered for. During one scan, the researchers' played Stravinsky's *Firebird*, a very exhilarating piece of music. They then played a piece from Tchaikovsky's *Swan Lake*. The *f*MRI discovered that during the much calmer composition, the song from *Swan Lake*, her brain was on fire with electrical reactions, but not during the more stimulating *Firebird*. Why? Because Svetlana had once danced in Swan Lake and felt closer to that composition. Every note evoked a familiar emotional, therefore neural, reaction. On a lesser scale, a familiar or less familiar word creates diverse neurotransmissions in your Quarry's brain.

Kids learn language by listening to their parents, relatives, friends, and other familiar folks around whom they feel comfortable. Phoneticists observe that there are not just regional differences in words and accents but that even people in different schools, groups, and parts of a city use ever-so-slightly different words.

Chemistry Sparker #41

Use Your Quarry's Words

To make your Quarry feel like you're on the same "wave-length," use the same words for anything or anyone. She might say, "my mother," "my mom," "my mama," or "my mommy." He might refer to "Dad," "Pop," "Poppa," or "my old man." Yet they can all live in the same neighborhood. Saying your Quarry's words for common things Sparks a subliminal LoveMap sense of familiarity and similarity.

So . . . How Should I Listen?

I've never actually been asked that question, but I thought I'd answer it anyway. A film of a man listening would, compared to that of a woman, look like a still life. A female's listening demeanor is closer to those toy-dunking ducks that kids balance on the side of a water glass. A man listens silently, but a woman nods to a soundtrack of trifling vocal interjections like "uh huh," "oh," "umm," and a selection of other supportive cooing sounds.

Sometimes when speaking to a male, I exasperatingly assume he's not hearing a word I say because he's as silent as a dead cell phone. I mentioned it to one guy, and he had the nerve to tell me my little "interruptions" were annoying. (Imagine that!)

Well, each gender is an expert on his own listening preferences, so to Spark similarity, go with your Quarry's flow.

Chemistry Sparker #42

Hunters, Listen with Nods and Supportive Sounds

Gentlemen, signal you are listening by sprinkling short murmurs of understanding between your Quarry's sentences. "Um, hum" is okay but could get repetitive. Practice vocalizing a few supportive comments concentrating on *emotion* words like: "I know how you must have *felt*," "I would have *sensed* the same thing," and "I *sympathize* with you."

Huntresses, the reverse . . .

♀ Chemistry Sparker #43

Huntresses, Don't Interject Emotional Affirmations

Shh, ladies. Squelch supportive cooing, which disturbs his concentration and also takes away from your seriousness. Give the guy time between sentences to think about his next. Only during obvious pauses should you interject a comment, perhaps a supportive statement. Try little kudos like, "That was smart of you," "Excellent," or "You did the right thing."

I Want a Man Who Makes Me Laugh

You've heard women lovingly say about a man, "He makes me laugh." But have you ever heard a man say, "She makes me laugh?" Not likely, unless he's putting her down. Look on any dating site and you'll see "good sense of humor" so often that it has merited an acronym, GSOH. The desirability of GSOH has been proven by herds of serious humor researchers (not an oxymoron). Hunters and Huntresses find very different things humorous.

Stanford researchers engaged ten males and ten females to lie down on a narrow examination table, individually, not as a group exercise. Each subject slid head first into a hole in a huge metal brain-scanning machine with a series of cartoons projected on the circular ceiling. The examiners then measured the subjects' internal giggle or guffaw by tracking what parts of their brains lit up—and how bright—at each cartoon.

What Makes Huntresses Laugh

The females reacted more slowly. It wasn't that they were slower to "get it." It's just that, after reading the caption, the women processed it through their stronger linguistic sense, then ran it by their prefrontal cortex to see if it really made sense. The more unexpected or incongruous the caption was, the funnier females found it.[9]

Huntresses don't enjoy canned humor. They prefer Hunters who can grasp the wit in an unexpected situation and play off it. It all goes back to the evolutionary female dictum to get the best partner.[10] Any old guy can memorize jokes. But picking up on an immediate occurrence, seeing the humor in it, and expressing it shows flexibility, intelligence, and cognitive fitness.[11]

Chemistry Sparker #44

Don't Tell Your Quarry Jokes

Hunters, save them for your friends, your compadres, your amigos, and your old buddy-roos. They'll love 'em. But definitely use off-the-cuff unexpected humor with women. Look on the light side of life and see something immediate and funny. Your clever comment will demonstrate your obvious superiority over all those other dull-witted Hunters vying for the lady's favors.

What Makes Hunters Laugh

Males, in their typically more rational, linear way of thinking, found the cartoons funnier faster. Why? Well, because they were cartoons. They were *supposed* to be funny. Guys love sitting around with a six-pack of beer telling jokes for competitive reasons too. May the best joke win! Some guys like sight gags. But women sense the truth: Even a gorilla laughs at another slipping on a banana peel.

Hunters and Huntresses, there are a multitude of ingenious ways to make your Quarry take the tumble on dates. I don't want to be repetitive, however, so for more tips, I'll refer you to my previous book, *How to Make Anyone Fall in Love with You.* There you'll find eighty-five ways to do that based on sociological studies and subtle persuasion techniques. Just promise me you'll play fair and won't misuse any of the "little tricks" therein!

CHAPTER 7

How to Spark Chemistry for Sex

Every author comes to a stumbling block when writing a book. Mine wasn't "writer's block." It was "shall I put this chapter in front of that one or the reverse?" block. When it came to Sex Sparkers and Love Sparkers, should I put sex before love, or love before sex?

If I wrote about sex before love, my mother would shake her fist and shout at me from heaven. In most of today's world, however, it is antiquated to say there has to be commitment before sex. Besides, for both Hunters and Huntresses the ideal Love Boat has the same final destination, lasting togetherness. Initial lust and falling in love are just two ports along the way. Depending on whether a Hunter or Huntress is at the helm, however, the boat takes a different route.

A male wants sex first, then fondness, then love.

A female wants fondness first, then love and sex together.

Huntresses, being choosier, usually need to like a guy a lot before sharing a pillow. Hunters want undercover activities right away. Considering this disparity, I couldn't decide which section, Love

Sparkers or Sex Sparkers, to put first. So I turned to my relationship seminar students to help with the decision.

One particular program I gave in Sioux City was perfect for the task. Not only was it in the politically early indicator state of Iowa, but there were also an almost equal number of male and female participants. I told the group about this upcoming book and begged their counsel.

I asked the class, "How many of you suggest I put the love section first?" About half the hands went up. Ninety percent of those hands looked suspiciously female. Everyone looked around and laughed, seeing how gender specific the choice was.

I continued, "How many think the sex part should come first?" Male hands shot up like fireworks, accompanied by a chorus of affirmatives. "Yeah," "Sure," "Definitely."

I got the point. We then dove into a discussion of lust and love. All of us wound up agreeing that the two are hard to separate, so we decided to toss a coin. Heads, Love. Tails, Sex. I flipped the coin high in the air and it came back . . . tails. The girls booed. The guys cheered.

I never defile the sacredness of the coin toss, so I will talk about sex before falling in love.

Huntresses, How Soon Should You Have Sex?

Here I go, sounding like Granny again, but having sex on one of the first few dates is not such a good idea for many reasons—and as you'll see, it's not just the obvious ones like "He'll think I'm cheap." The suggestion of holding off on sex for a while sounds retro to you, right? After all, this is the twenty-first century. We know the steps to (somewhat) prevent STDs and unwanted pregnancy. So what's wrong with it?

Girl, when you and a guy hop into bed and go at it, his testosterone shoots up off the charts, and his pleasure center gets drunk with dopamine. Just as he's coming, the bonding chemical, oxytocin, goes up 500 percent.[1] In fact, that's the moment a man might blurt out, "I love you" to a woman he doesn't actually love. But for those few seconds, he feels he really does.

But then, *poof*, after ejaculation, testosterone plunges, along with the "I love you" chemical.[2] His dopamine crashes after coming, and the blast knocks him out. Snoring soon follows. (I hear you, girl-friend. We'll talk about his devastating not-wanting-to-cuddle condition later.) Your man's postcoital flushed face on the pillow might mumble, "Give me an hour or so, honey, and I'll be ready to go again." And he may well be able to do that. But of course, it won't be as exciting for him as the first time.

But here's what most Huntresses don't understand. *Unless he's already started to develop feelings for you,* sex with you won't be as thrilling for him the next night—or the next—or the next—or even a week later! You could be the most exciting woman he ever met. But that extraordinary dopamine surge, like anything else that feels good, becomes less sensitive to the identical stimulus the second time, third time, and so forth. If a Hunter is having a lot of sex with the same woman (unless he's already developed feelings for her), she has to keep raising the bar. And a Huntress can only go so far with new erotic contortions, creativity, and sex toys.

One particular experiment made this dismal fact exceedingly clear.[3] Researchers put a particular species of male lab rat into a cage with a new female. The duo indulged in a round-the-clock, nonstop orgy until the poor male zonked out, drowning in sweat and gasping for breath. But no matter how much time passed, he wasn't in the least bit interested in going at it again with the same female.

However, when the researchers introduced a new lady into the cage, the lucky rat became ravenous again and hopped all over her. The experiment was repeated, and sure enough, the little guy could always get it up for a new girl in the cage. But the previous night's one-night stand was ho-hum.

To quote one of the landmark studies, "Sexually satiated males cease copulating after several ejaculations with the same female; and the presence of an unknown receptive female renews copulation including ejaculation."[4] This became known throughout the science world as the "Coolidge effect."

"Why Coolidge?" you ask. Well, one fine day, while inspecting a government farm, the President and Mrs. Coolidge were on separate tours. When Mrs. Coolidge passed the chicken pens, she spotted a rooster having sex. She inquired if the rooster copulates more than once each day. "Dozens of times," replied the guide.

"Please tell that to the president," Mrs. Coolidge requested.

When the president later passed the pens and was told about the rooster, he asked, "Same hen every time?"

"Oh no, Mr. President, a different one each time."

The president nodded slowly, then said, "Tell that to Mrs. Coolidge."[5]

Laboratory rodents have a similar limbic system to human rats (and human nice guys as well), so they provide some pretty trustworthy evidence. Having sex with a man *before* he starts to have feelings for you is not going to whet his appetite as much as wither it. Of course, *after* he's starting to fall in love with you, it's an entirely different story. He can't get enough of you and would rather be in bed with you than any other woman in the world.

Why Sex Blows Your Mind

It makes sense that sex packs a pretty powerful punch because orgasm involves more areas of the brain than any other activity, short of an epileptic seizure.[6] Your amygdala is in an emotional frenzy and commands your hippocampus, *Mr. Memory,* to forget everything and just enjoy it. Your hypothalamus, *Mr. Action,* kicks your whole body into a frenetic carnal dance. Meanwhile the various brain precincts are hollering at mission control, your prefrontal cortex, to chill and not think about anything.

All the sex chemicals are going bonkers. Testosterone swirls around with estrogen. Dopamine and his helpers have a wild party on *Pleasure Island* (your caudate nucleus), which flashes like a strobe. Oxytocin and vasopressin light the fuse and explode at orgasm. No wonder sex is a BIG deal and blows your mind!

Huntresses, Sex Has an Even Bigger Effect on You!

Be careful, girl. Although men are more ravenous for sex as soon as possible, it has a stronger and longer-lasting impact on you. The powerful physiological effect from all those chemicals you release can persist for weeks, even months. If you don't feel a particular man is totally right for you, be careful, because the dopamine and oxytocin blast of sex can make you think you're in love with him.[7] One of the most respected sex researchers in the world tells women in her lectures, "Don't have sex with any man you're not prepared to fall in love with."[8] Oxytocin has the phenomenal effect of creating trust and flushing out bad memories, closing your eyes to the fact that he's a creep.[9]

The chemical's loving power was made very evident in one particular study in which subjects, half of whom were given oxytocin and half a placebo, were asked to recall their early childhood experiences with their mothers.[10] The oxytocin sniffers talked much more highly of Mom. They described her being warmer and more loving than the placebo sniffers. Oxytocin even suppresses memories of bad experiences.

Now I'm the one to say, "It happened to me, dearie, it can happen to you." I once felt that Spark of instant Chemistry for a suave Spaniard named Santos. He had an electrifying air of mystery about him, and I fell into his bed much too quickly. I believed Santos was a man of morality and high standards. He went to church regularly and spoke often of his spirituality. Many of his stories underscored his commitment to truth and his honesty. He seemed ideal. Sex was wonderful, and I was smitten.

Then one or two trivial matters sent up a tiny red flag. Santos had his caller ID blocked for outgoing calls, which I've never liked on anyone's phone. That was minor, though. Whenever I called from my cell, he'd pick up with a quick, "Hi Babe." But the few times I called him from another phone with a number unrecognizable to him, he didn't even say "hello" until I spoke first. Apparently Santos didn't want to identify himself until he knew who was on the other end of the line. I was so in love with him, though, I didn't give it a second thought.

I closed my eyes to other small indications that he might not be the honorable man I thought him to be. Whenever he got in his car, he assiduously turned on the radar detector and even attached it to my car when we rode in it. I found that a little strange because he never sped. Why was he so concerned about being stopped by the police?

Once we were going to have lunch at a diner, and driving into the parking lot, he saw several police cars parked in front of it. He made an abrupt U-turn. When I asked him why, he said he thought it was unethical that police are sometimes given free food and didn't want to witness such a disgrace. I assumed that was because he was so highly principled. But then a few drops of doubt began to splash on the cement.

His sister came to New York for a visit, and during dinner she told me there was "a period of several years when nobody knew where Santos was." He just shrugged and said he'd had a falling out with his dad and didn't let the family know his whereabouts. I didn't like that, and my blinders started to slip.

Then came the incident that ripped them off entirely. Santos was coming to my apartment for dinner at seven. While cooking, I looked out my kitchen window and saw someone on the fire escape across the courtyard jimmying up a neighbor's window. I had just hung up from 911 when Santos arrived. When I told him the police were on the way, he went ballistic. My beloved Dr. Jekyll suddenly turned into a vitriolic Mr. Hyde. Shouting at me that he didn't like "snooping cops," he stormed out the door, leaving me devastated.

In my wounded state I started piecing together some of Santos's actions that, at the time, I had thought nothing of. First his refusal to say "hi" on the phone until he knew who was calling. Then his obsessive use of the radar detector for police cars. Later the avoidance of the diner where law enforcement officers were dining. Why hadn't I seen the evidence mounting that he was hiding something from the police? I subsequently discovered he was, and it was pretty serious.

I wish I'd known at the time what researchers in the psychology of love have discovered. To quote one of the leading researchers in love, "Newly smitten lovers often idealize their partner, magnifying their virtues and explaining away their flaws."[11] That's what happened to me. The chemicals saturating my brain had clouded clear vision.

Sometimes, when I'd hear about people who'd had a bitter divorce, I used to wonder how good people who used to love each other could possibly wind up with such rancor. Now I understand. They thought it was love, but it was merely being "in love," which is an entirely different neurochemical state. The couples tragically didn't wait to see if it was real love, the kind that generates different chemicals—the ones we'll talk about in Chapter 10—which last a lot longer and bring continued happiness. Don't let sex or the craving of it with one particular person make you think you're in love. Because love, until it's stood the test of time, really is blind.

♀ Chemistry Sparker #45

Scrap Sex on the First Couple of Dates

Huntresses, wait until your Quarry has feelings for you before having sex or else he can lose interest. A lot of old wives' tales are false, but this one is a neurochemical and biological fact.

Sex too early screws up your life in other ways too—and not in ways that have anything to do with pregnancy, morality, or physical health. The sex chemicals in your brain could make you inadvertently do or say things that might mess up a potentially great relationship. Worse, it could make you think you're in love with a louse like it did me.

Hunters, Hints for You on First-Date Sex

Gentlemen, I know this is going to fall on deaf ears, but sex on the first couple of dates is not such a good idea for you either. The oxytocin that momentarily streams through your brain at orgasm could make you say something you don't mean, like the "L" word. But please, Hunters, bite your tongue—which is kind of hard to do just before coming—and don't say anything untrue that could later hurt her. The lingering chemical could also trigger her trust circuits so much that she might not realize it if you're trying to edge out of the relationship. Men in my seminars have told me about girlfriends who, when they tried to move on, just didn't "get it." Putting it more selfishly, gentlemen, you don't want a stalker on your hands! Play fair.

Here's another strike against first-date sex: After a big slug of the testosterone/dopamine cocktail, your brain can't possibly see the more subtle aspects of a woman's personality clearly. Having your mind blown by hot sex before you've even gotten to know her could blind you to a pretty terrific lady who could someday mean a lot more to you than one hot night.

(Hmm, if the word got out that I was suggesting not trying for sex on the first date, no males would buy the book.) Don't hate me for saying this guys, but think about not pressuring her for sex too soon. In the long run it's better for both of you.

Let's move on to subsequent dates, when sex is most likely in the picture. You probably know women want longer foreplay, but you have absolutely no idea how long! You may think it all starts when the two of you hit the sack, the couch, the floor, the wherever. Wrong. For her, foreplay began many hours, days, or even weeks before.[12]

Foreplay Begins Way Long Before the Bedroom

Dear Hunters, I hope you don't take offense at the following. When it comes to giving women incredible orgasms, however, some men need a few insights and, well, a map. It's not your fault. Males are not as intuitive due to the natural neuroanatomical reasons mentioned before. Additionally, a woman often hesitates to give her man verbal or geographical directions for fear of hurting his feelings.

Gentlemen, during sex the lady has an infallible gauge on your ecstasy. Your sexual "meter" can't lie. Determining her real erotic gratification is, however, a bigger challenge for a guy-type brain. Maybe you've been keeping track of what makes her moan the most or scream the loudest. Among all of earth's miraculous creatures, a human being is the only one capable of being a conscious performer in bed. Your Quarry probably suffers from an untreatable female condition: the desire to please and make others feel good about themselves—a quality that someday you will deeply appreciate.

When a woman is falling in love with you, she's every bit as ravenous for sex as you, many times even more so. She thinks about it all the time and walks around in a state of sexual frenzy. However, when the big moment comes, it takes longer for her to push everything out of her mind and warm up.[13] Her feelings and responses—past, present, and fantasies of the future—play a major role in her enjoyment of sex.

When you meet her at the door, she may have no idea whether she'll want sex with you at the end of the evening. She waits to see if it "feels right" at the time. Everything depends on her memories and moment-to-moment reactions to you—some momentous, some minor. Minutiae like the following can make the difference between major lovemaking and a quick "G'nite." How respectful were you to her when you picked her up this evening? Did you take a long cell phone call at the table? Were you rude to the waiter? Did you leave a decent tip?

"What's *that* got to do with sex?" you ask. A lot, because if her hippocampus, which has a close relationship with her emotional amygdala, harbors any negative memories of the evening, sex is no-go. Unlike you, she can't box up her feelings in one brain region with no leakage. There is permanent seepage between relationship issues and sex.[14] Whether your date with her ends horizontally or vertically can depend on what you'd call trivia. From the moment you meet at the rendezvous point, you must make her feel special throughout the whole evening.

With that in mind, let's skip to the end of the date that you hope will culminate in a lot more than a goodnight kiss.

Set the Stage for Sex

Neither gender can enjoy sex if preoccupied by other matters.[15] However, you gentlemen have the enviable capability of turning your amygdala off like a single lamp on the night table and getting right into action. Your Quarry, conversely, has a slow dimmer on hers. It's up to you to bring it from its usual overactive brilliance down to dark romantic lighting, psychologically and physically. The key word is s-l-o-w-l-y.

An uncomfortable setting can also spark or park her desire for sex. If you even suspect she might grace your pad with her presence at the end of the evening, fling any previously worn clothes on the closet floor. Then close the door—tight. A woman is much more sensitive to the sense of smell.[16] Tell your grungy socks to scurry under the bed, and figure out how to turn on the vacuum cleaner your mother gave you two birthdays ago.

Finally, do an atmosphere check. Is the room too stuffy? Is it too hot, too cold? Did you know most women can't fully enjoy sex if their feet are cold?[17] Seriously. Will your Quarry feel the lights are too bright? There are reasons she might fear this that you could never fathom—like will you see her cellulite or smeared makeup? She can't let herself go and enjoy sex if she's freaking about things like that. What about the music? Does she like jazz, classical, country, heavy metal, or Nordic folk? When in doubt, ask her.

Chemistry Sparker #46

Hunters, Set the Stage for Sex Ahead of Time

To a Huntress, the setting can mean the difference between "yes" and "no." Do some preplanning before you arrive at your place with your Quarry. Your best bet is dim lighting, pleasant-smelling air, and a soft, previously made bed. Check the pillows for any long hairs, and turn off the spotlight by your bed. She's at your pad, not the gynecologist's.

When It's Time to Get Naked

Once again, the key word is s-l-o-w-l-y. Instant stark nudity is not a turn-on for your Quarry. Some plucky researchers hooked females up to a vaginal photoplethysmograph to measure their vasoengorgement. (Don't ask what that is. Look it up if you're really interested.) It turns out that they were no more excited by videos of naked men than they were by naked women. In fact, women preferred panoramas of the snowcapped Himalayas to nude males.[18]

For several years, while doing corporate consulting in Bermuda, I dated a brilliant executive there named Niles whenever I was on the island. Even though I really liked him, I had never agreed to sex.

But holding hands with him across the table at lunch one day, I realized the foolishness of my ways. "Niles," I purred, "I have something for you." Reaching into my purse, I took an extra key card to my hotel room and placed it on the table in front of him. He took both my hands and told me how happy he was.

Niles said he'd get there early, before I got back from an evening seminar, and would order room service for us. In the taxi on the way back to the hotel that night, I wondered what wine he had ordered for our predinner toast. Riding up in the elevator, I pondered what aroma would be rising through the little hole in the plate cover when I walked into the room. I'd had a hard time concentrating on my seminar during the day because I couldn't keep my mind off how wonderful sex was going to be with him that night. Excitedly, I slid my card into the lock and entered. The lights were out, but the full moon shining through the lace drapery gave a glow to the room. How exquisitely romantic!

As my eyes got used to the light though, instead of a room service table set for two, there was a naked Niles stretched on the bed with his arms behind his head. "You can see that I've been waiting for you," he said huskily, referring to his excitement meter pointing straight up. I apologized profusely and feigned a splitting headache. After I practically pushed him out the door, I went down to the hotel pub, had a big hamburger, and swore never to see him again.

Until recently I feared my aversion to his no-foreplay nudity might be abnormal and that I was the perverse one, not he. I was relieved while reading the plethora of studies confirming it was a normal female reaction. Niles wasn't abnormal either. It's just that he wasn't in the know about a woman needing more time to get in the mood.

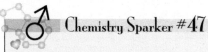

Chemistry Sparker #47

Let Her Start the Strip

Hunters, don't you start peeling. After an appropriate length of time, if she hasn't, start gently with a button on her blouse or perhaps your shirt. But keep your hands away from your belt until it's obvious the feeling is mutual. Grabbing for your buckle can make her grab for her coat.

Oral Sex (It's Not What You're Thinking)

If the lady has extended the invitation to join her for a nightcap, do not pounce on her the moment she sits down. Start with a few caring moves, perhaps touching her cheek or brushing the hair out of her face. Now it's time to get "oral," as in "talking." It's tough because a guy's lack of ability to process emotions and say just right thing at the right time was formed in his mother's womb.[19] It's hard for a guy's brain to wrap itself around the fact that words mean so much to his Quarry, so let me suggest a few phrases. Note, I did not say lines or lies! After all, if you didn't feel one of the following sentiments, you wouldn't be sitting next to the lady.

Chemistry Sparker #48

Don't Get Physical, Get Verbal

Words work wonders on your Quarry's need to calm down before heating up. Gaze deeply into her eyes and talk softly to the lady. Let her know how lovely she looks, how fascinating you find her, how happy you are that you are together tonight. Verbal foreplay is sexier to her than passionate pawing.

The Educational Value of Daytime Soaps

Likewise, Hunters, you'll get priceless insights into your Quarry's fantasies by watching a daytime TV soap opera gushing with strong, sensitive, respectful—yet sometimes recklessly passionate—males. One guy friend told me he learned "the killer kiss" from the *Young and the Restless*. He said, "The dude cupped the woman's face in his hands and gave her a light kiss on the nose. Smiling, he pulled back and gently outlined her lips with his finger. Then he told her how beautiful she was and enveloped her in his arms."

Sigh.

Just to make it more complicated, no two women are alike in precisely what they want once the action begins.

"Oh, Great, How Do I Find Out What She Really Wants?"

Gentlemen, go with your strong suit, your gray matter. Simply ask her. Choose a tranquil time, preferably one when sex is not in the immediate picture. Say something like, "You look especially beautiful when you're so relaxed." Lead the conversation around to the question, "What physically relaxes you the most?" She might say something like a warm bath, a back rub, a foot massage. Whatever it is, tell *Mr. Memory* to store it away and remind you when it becomes pertinent. Then, when the time comes try to arrange her favorite atmosphere.

I fell prey, blissfully, once to what might have called a ploy. But looking back, I don't care. It was lovely. Josh and I had been dating for a while, and at one point, while sitting on the couch, he took my hand tenderly and said, "Leil, please forgive me if this is an improper question. But have you ever considered having sex with me?" I didn't tell him that I'd thought about little else since we met. I managed a demure smile and a shy, tentative "yes."

Josh squeezed my hand and continued. "If I should be so lucky, how would it happen?" I melted like an ice cube under a blow torch. He teasingly asked me if I'd like music, what kind of wine, lighting. It seemed so sweet and silly that I started giggling. But on our next date everything was in place. And because of that, so was I.

Chemistry Sparker #49

Ask Her to Describe Her Secret Garden

Hunters, I hesitate recommending this approach unless you feel confident you can carry it off, but I do want to give testimony to its efficacy. Lovingly—and with perhaps a touch of humor—ask her what she thinks is the perfect atmosphere for "making love." (Forget you ever heard the word "sex.") Then have it all set up the next time you see her.

Why She Needs All That Stuff First

When I was a kid, Mama gave me amazing birthday parties. The best one of all was a breakfast birthday with waffles and four different kinds of syrups—strawberry, blueberry, raspberry, and maple. All the kids, about ten of us, were wide-eyed when Mama triumphantly carried in an almost two-foot-high stack of waffles. The girls clapped and the boys grabbed at the treat.

One of the oldest boys assiduously poured strawberry syrup in one of the squares. He then proceeded to spill blueberry in the next, raspberry in another, maple in a fourth. All the other guys thought it was cool and followed suit. We girls, however, mixed them together and made our own creative blends of several syrups. We then passed our plates around the table to share our concoctions with our friends. The boys weren't interested and continued to concentrate on dispensing syrups into the different squares.

Squares versus Swirls

A grownup guy does that with his life. His job goes in one little waffle square, sports in another, and sex in yet another. No problem. But here's the rub: In order to enjoy sex, *both* Hunters and Huntresses alike need to make it an all-consuming experience and think of nothing else. Gentlemen, if you couldn't stop thinking about your boss hollering at you this morning, the SOB who got the promotion instead of you, or the power outage during your big PowerPoint presentation, how could you get it up for sex? The difference is that when sex is in the picture, you can instantly chuck garbage like that out of your mind and jump into a different waffle square.

Your Quarry can't. It's neurologically impossible. Only when she suppresses memories and extinguishes her other thoughts can she thoroughly enjoy sex.[20] Just as the girls at my birthday party had no dividing lines between their syrups and swirled them all together, we grownup girls blend all the elements in our adult lives.

Hunters, your Quarry needs time to clear out all that crappy real-life stuff. Otherwise, the mean boss and the bitch who beat her out at work are right there in bed with the two of you. The power outage during her presentation darkens her desire. Because a woman is more relationship oriented, everything you said to her today, yesterday, and last week swirls into her desire to have sex with you—or not.

Think of a Huntress's brain like a big dish of pasta. It's all interconnected. If the sex noodle is at the bottom of the bowl, she can't pull it out without several other gummy noodles sticking to it. And if you try to separate them too fast, you'll have more success playing pickup sticks with cooked spaghetti strings. If you really want your Quarry to forget everything and get into sex, you must clear her mind with caring words and caresses all over her body.

"But I don't have time to do that every time!" you protest. I understand, Hunters. But stay tuned. All will become clear.

Women Don't Come with Pull-Down Menus and Online Help

Your caring words create the bonding chemical oxytocin, and your caresses create even more of that precious element, especially when you kiss her breasts. I don't expect you to find anything titillating about reading the *Gynecologic and Obstetric Investigation* journal, so I'll translate. Studies on female sexual arousal stress the importance of fondling her breasts. It's not just because it feels good; they're a regular oxytocin factory because her breasts are the big deal in baby feeding.[21]

When it comes to love, oxytocin is huge for a female. Mother Nature doles out a major dose to her during pregnancy and then a whopping three hundred times more of it at childbirth. That attachment chemical just keeps on coming and coming during nursing and beyond. As a result, through thick and thin, Mom will forever bond with the little person who started in her womb. The togetherness chemical also makes her want to bond with you and have even more sex together.

Female skin is more sensitive and sensual all over than a man's. Hunters, comparatively, your body is a single-destination trip. She, however, has multiple sexual layover spots along the way. A different part of her brain lights up with each one. You exploring a much vaster territory stimulates her *Pleasure Island*, and playing around on each part takes time.

Rutgers researchers—rather cheeky ones I must say—put women into an *f*MRI machine with nothing but a dildo for company. The ladies wound up using it and their hands on four parts of their bodies—nipples, cervix, vagina, and clitoris.[22] Sometimes all four at once. But the clitoris was always involved.

Who Stole the G-Spot?

Unfortunately, a woman often feels it's her fault if she can't orgasm with no male attention to her clitoris, condescendingly referred to by Freud and Co. as the "little penis." I was once discussing this distressing situation with a few of my girlfriends, and each confessed that she never gave her boyfriend a thorough geography lesson lest he feel his technique was being questioned.

"And while we're at it," my best friend, Stella, piped up, "I've never been able to find that darn G-spot that every woman in the world has except me." I explained that Dr. Ernst Gräfenberg was the person, male of course, who pushed it to stardom in the 1950s, claiming women had a vaginal climax separate from a clitoral. (Apparently Mrs. Gräfenberg never spoke up.) For decades afterward medical examiners conducting autopsies scratched their heads wondering why the G-spot mysteriously disappeared posthumously.

They never found it because it never existed as the orgasmic gizmo it was reputed to be.[23] So if coroners burrowing around in there with expensive equipment couldn't find it, don't depend on it giving her ultimate pleasure without equally attending to her hottest spot of all, the "C-spot"—the clitoris.

♂ Chemistry Sparker #50

Master Geography 101 for Hunters

Women joke about how territorially challenged some men are when it comes to the female body. She is probably lying if she claims she can climax from vaginal entry alone without any contact with her clitoris. Ask your girlfriend for a geography lesson to her particular body because each female is slightly different. Once she's gratefully given you a personal tour of her unique favorite spots, be sure to give each lots of lengthy tender, loving care.

Sisters, a quick note for you: A softer way to guide him through the southern regions is simply to say, "I especially love it when you touch me here, or there—or both at the same time." It sounds obvious, but you'd be surprised how many women shy away from doing this.

Huntresses Are Naturals

Huntresses, you are more romantically intuitive than males are, and you're natural pleasers. Not only that but you'll find scads of information everywhere you turn. Unfortunately, one of the most popular sources of information is *Cosmopolitan* magazine, published in twenty-eight countries in sixteen languages. An issue I came across gives instructions for running her tongue around the rim of her boyfriend's penis while stroking his balls with her left hand and insinuating her right index finger up his anus. I am not making this up!

Am I putting this invaluable font of knowledge down? Not really. My only regret is that although *Cosmo*'s published demographics start at eighteen, young girls now give a subscription to their girlfriends for their sweet sixteen parties. Ouch. The implication that all girls are having sex with their beau du jour and the lack of warnings about the psychological and physiological perils of promiscuity are pretty scary. My feminist side also fears the geisha mentality it imparts. That aside (and it's a pretty big aside), it is indeed informative in the gymnastics and erotic toys departments.

One *Cosmo* feature was especially enlightening. The title was "Thirty Things to Do with a Naked Man," and the subtitle touted, "Sex Tips to Tease, Squeeze, and Totally Please Your Guy."[24] The editorial advised young ladies to employ blindfolds in bed, frozen grapes in her mouth, Velcro restraints, gladiator heels, Gummi bears, sushi rolls, small mirrors, and a beaded necklace as a penis wrap.

Of course, accoutrements are not always necessary. It informs the young reader that she can "intensify his orgasm by placing two fingers an inch behind his balls and feeling for a dent" or "invite him to finish on your breasts." Another suggestion is to "challenge" him to have sex in five spots in your apartment before sundown.

I have no problem with any of the above. (However, your male Quarry might with that last one.) In fact, sex toys and erotic contortions are fabulous fun during the period when Mother Nature is still plying the new lovers with drugs. Sex is a mind-blowing turn-on for a Huntress, and she can't get enough of her guy. The Sparks on *Pleasure Island* spread like a brush fire on a windy day just knowing the thrills she's giving her Quarry and how much he'll love her for creative and strenuous gymnastics. It's action for a cause.

In the natural course of a relationship, however, a Huntress would tire of doing all that work. Additionally, if she's pushed the relationship too fast, it might dawn on her Quarry that he could get like favors from a less long-term, more munificent lady. He's thinking, "I could get these benefits without her always asking me where our relationship is going or freaking if I even look at another girl."

Go Where Women Aren't Allowed

Lasting Chemistry and true love don't come from doggy-style, convoluted Indian–style, or even Viennese oyster–style sex. It's not finding that dent or luxuriating in his essences all over your breasts. Fun stuff aside—or included—in order to get some long-term neural activity going, you need to go beyond the beaded necklaces and blindfolds. You must delve into the most erotic part of the body: his brain, of course.

Let's discuss what his hundred billion neurons are up to while having sex. Until he's fallen deeply in love with you, a Hunter usually suspends relationship thoughts during the act. In fact, if he feels the "situation" softening a bit, he consciously switches gears, invoking hot memories of a previous encounter, perhaps a woman he spotted on the street today, a threesome, foursome, or more-some.[25] Or perhaps just visions of isolated breasts, genitals, and other favored female body parts dance through his head.

What kind of fantasies does he have? Well, let's see. How many stars are in the sky? How many angels can dance on the head of a pin? How many pickled peppers did Peter Piper pick? Sexual fantasies are as varied as the males who have them.[26]

Out of perverse curiosity, one time I asked an ex-boyfriend, who later became a buddy, if I could scrounge through the dusty stack of old porn magazines and videos he confessed he'd hidden under the bed. In the box that he'd labeled "extra blanket" I unearthed a gold mine of information about what men really find hot, and it's not frozen grapes and Gummi bears. One magazine was simply a selection of stories about sexy showgirls, naughty nurses, and warrior vixens. If you know the types of things your Quarry is fantasizing about during sex and embrace it, you're caressing his hottest organ by far—his brain.

To get an authentic education on the male sexual psyche, start perusing mild men's mags like *Penthouse* and *Playboy*. Then if you can stomach it, graduate (or sink to) reading *Mayfair* and *Club International*. After hitting rock bottom with *Barely Legal*, you'll either be an expert on men's fantasies or decide to become a lesbian.

♀ Chemistry Sparker #51

Read What *He* Reads for Hot Hints

Why read about what turns your Quarry on in magazines written by females? Forget *Cosmo*. Read the real story in the rags written by and for men. I'd also suggest visiting a few online porn sites, but the viruses, spyware, tracking cookies, Trojans, and other social-media transmitted diseases could be injurious to your computer's health.

Better Yet, Get It Straight from the Horse's Mouth

Huntresses, in order to excavate sexual buried treasure he's never shared with anyone, find a way to bring up the subject of erotic fantasies. Perhaps with a wink, let him know you find the topic titillating. Maybe tell him you were reading an article or book on them. (But not this one!) Better yet, reveal one of your own fantasies—being taken by a handsome stranger, doing it in the airplane lavatory—the usual stuff. The hotter, the better.

After your "big confession," casually ask if he has any fantasies. That's a rhetorical question, because of course he does. If he says, "All I think about is you," that's sweet, but he's lying. Keep probing. Secretly, he'll love it. Let him know *nothing* would shock you.

At that point your Quarry may surreptitiously look around, lean forward, and most likely confess a mundane fantasy—which he feels is monstrous. The most common male fantasies are having sex with two women, watching them get it on with each other, or a little dab of dominance.[27] Your playful smile and hearing, "ooh, that's exciting" floods his pleasure center with a tsunami of dopamine. That plus the torrent of testosterone create the perfect storm.

♀ Chemistry Sparker #52

Conduct an Erotic Interview

Ask your Quarry what he fantasizes about during sex. After he recovers from the delicious shock of your question, he will be thrilled because you're probably the first female requesting entry into that tangled exotic erotic universe where anything goes. The neural pathways connecting you to his *Pleasure Island* will open up like a superhighway.

"Does that mean I have to perform with another woman or wear a corset and crack a whip?" you ask. Of course not. Most women have had "rape fantasies." But that's the last thing they'd really want!

If his fantasy happens to be something you would enjoy doing, however, like wearing hot lingerie or stockings to bed, go for it. Just be prepared that his fantasy could be *him* wearing the stockings and hot lingerie to bed! Unless you find it distasteful, letting him do his sex dream is the hottest sex Sparker in existence. It's the ultimate in sexy for him because *he* wrote the script. Just keep in mind that doing his fantasy is usually not a one-night performance. If you're serious about the chap, you better decide if you'd like a lifetime of it. His tying you to the bedpost or wearing your panties as foreplay could go from big turn-on to turn-off.

Why Won't He Cuddle After Sex?

Rock stars, cinema heart throbs, or the Quarry we just met often pop into a female's sexual fantasies. But when we're in bed with a particular man, our erotica generally centers on him.[28]After the lovemaking, we rerun the tape of what he did, what he didn't do, and what we wish he'd done—and end by wishing he'd be more affectionate after sex.

My heart goes out to the many millions—no, the majority—of women like my friend Brandy who still thinks that if a man doesn't cuddle after sex it means he doesn't care for her. I now hope to dispel that myth once and for all with chemical evidence that it's not true.

I tried to tell Brandy that a guy is neurologically cuddle-challenged, but she wouldn't listen. I wanted to explain that the big blast of oxytocin released during orgasm affects the male brain like a sleeping pill. It's a universal male condition called "postcoital narcolepsy." When mixed with other sex chemicals, they produce an essence similar to melatonin, which plays a big role in a human's body clock.[29] It's a tall order for a man to stay awake after sex and has nothing at all to do with how much he cares for you.

In one of my seminars I was talking about how women adored hearing loving words after sex and quoted a few romance novels.

"My darling girl, I want to hold you forever."

"I am in heaven when I'm holding you."

"I could die of happiness in your arms like this."

Then, just for fun, I asked the men in the class if they had any favorite postcoital phrases for their girlfriends to suggest to the other guys. Blank faces stared back at me from all over the room.

"Uh, well, what you usually say?" I queried.

After a brief pause one guy raised his hand and said, "Zzzzzzzz." The guys hooted and slapped their knees. The girls grimaced and nodded all too knowingly.

♀ Chemistry Sparker #53

Let Him Have His Instantaneous Postsex Snooze

The second a Hunter comes, it's like he's popped an Ambien. When he zonks out it does not mean he wouldn't like to hold and kiss you. He biologically practically can't! Complaining, accusing, or insisting on snuggle time is not going to help your relationship. Just cuddle up against your chemically challenged animal and get forty winks yourself.

The more evolutionarily curious among you might well ask why nature makes a male suffer this condition. (Although it's usually the girlfriend or wife who suffers the most.) Big Mama in the sky's reason for knocking him out after sex is because he can't kick Charlie into action for a second round right away. But if he has a rejuvinating little snooze, he might get it up for another shot at a tiny new earth dweller.

Do You Decide Who Turns You On—or Does Mother Nature?

Here's another little known fact about sex. Sometimes your relationship was just not meant to be, and Mother Nature lets you know in no uncertain terms during the first kiss.

Hunters, let's say the first date with her went beautifully. She was more alluring, affectionate, and fun than you could ever have hoped for. As you rowed the rented rowboat, she admired your muscles. In fact, you both were enjoying yourselves so much that you brought the boat back late. But you handled it beautifully. After the owner tied up the boat, you crossed his wet palm with some significant green. He thanked you profusely and she looked up at you admiringly. It was the perfect date. She shared your interests, was impressed by your subtle but intelligent humor, and even ordered the same pizza at the pub. You think maybe she is "the one." By her warmth you can tell she probably feels the same.

Back on her doorstep, she leans seductively toward you. You know she is cranked for your kiss. As your lips touch, she parts hers, inviting your tongue to enter. You oblige.

Suddenly she stiffens and pushes you away. With a weak excuse, she races into her house. You're shell-shocked. What happened? Everything seemed so perfect. "What did I do wrong?" you ask yourself.

Huntresses, your date rings the bell. You take one last look in the mirror, splash a dab of perfume behind each ear, run down the stairs, and throw open the door. Wow, he's hotter than you remember him when you met him last week! You know you look awesome too. You see intelligence, warmth, and humor in his eyes. The evening is magic. You talk 'til dawn. You think you've found "the one" and suspect he feels it too.

Later, just before sunrise, in the car he starts nibbling on your neck and you tenderly guide his head down to your cleavage. You arch your back and throw your head back. God, he feels good.

But suddenly he sits up, gives you a weak smile, a peck on the cheek, and revs up the car. You are flabbergasted. What happened? Everything seemed so perfect. "What did I do wrong?" you ask yourself.

Neither of you did anything wrong! But Mother Nature was not happy. And when Big Mama's not happy, nobody's happy. So why didn't she want the two of you to be a couple? Because she figured your eventual kid might not live up to her survival standards.

"What? How in the world did she deduce that?" you ask.

If the First Kiss Stinks, Forget About It

Everyone has a unique cluster of chromosomes that control the ability to fight off infections and disease. The tiny parasites in every human body reproduce faster than rabbits, and the germy little bastards are just waiting to attack your immune system. If you copulate with someone with similar bacteria, the stinky little slime balls join forces and will be victorious over your eventual baby's immune system.[30] It's the reason brothers and sisters and other close relatives shouldn't mate. Twenty years later, if the little tyke with the feeble immune system lives that long, he or she won't be able to produce healthy babies either. Mother Nature doesn't like that one bit. So she uses her Chemistry set to make the smell or saliva of your date distasteful to you if your microbes are too much alike.[31]

I was once explaining this phenomenon, called your Major Histocompatibility Complex (MHC), in a relationship seminar. Feeling insulted, one student shot up his hand and said, "Hey, I ain't got no complexes." I assured him that MHC is not a complex. It's a universal biological state.

I hate to reference the following tasteless, overly publicized study because it's such an old coin that the buffalo has worn off. But it's sort of unforgettable. Researchers convinced women to sniff a selection of guys' grungy T-shirts they'd worn for a week.[32.] It turns out the women actually liked the underarm aroma of guys with a *dissimilar* smell, or MHC. ('Fess up, sisters, haven't you ever slept with some article of your boyfriend's clothing when he was away?) But the T-shirt stink of guys who had a fragrance too similar to their own, like a family member's, grossed them out. That's why the smell of opposite sex siblings doesn't turn most people on sexually.

Far sweeter than any perfume is the natural odor of a sexual partner who has a different odor from yours. I'm not talking about flatulence, halitosis, or foot odor. I'm talking the hairy sweaty body parts, the fragrance of which is revealed through apocrine glands. Well, let's call a spade a spade and say it: It's your groin and armpits. These pits routinely spit out a lot of important internal social information.

A woman perceives odors better than a man does, and it's not just so she can tell when her baby's diaper is full. Because she's the real mate chooser, she needs to be extra skilled at literally sniffing guys out.[33] But watch out—she can also get a whiff of your stinky feet a couple yards away.

Gentlemen, your Quarry might appreciate your favorite over-the-counter man scent when you first meet. It shows you are clean and take care of your appearance. But between the sheets she responds better to the aroma of raw (clean) male. A Hunter is less sensitive to this aromatic matter on the first kiss because he's thinking of what's to come with the rest of her body. "Why let a little unsavory scent get in the way of a good thing?" he figures.

When searching for a sexually compatible partner, French kissing is a great test. White-fronted parrots have an ever better one. After the birds open their beaks and touch tongues, the male spews his lunch onto the female's chest.[34]

You really needed to know that, didn't you?

Huntresses, if your Quarry doesn't pass the taste test, no matter how much you adore him, he's not the right partner for you. Hunters, her fragrance may not be a big problem now, but sex with her in the long run could be odious. This is one time both of you should say, "Thanks, Mother Nature, for letting us know it wouldn't be a marriage made in heaven."

I hope the fragrance industry doesn't employ a slew of litigious attorneys, because the following Chemistry hint could ruin a good ROI on their annual advertising millions.

♀♂ Chemistry Sparker #54

Don't Wear the Smell-Good Stuff During Sex

Huntresses, males get high on your natural smell. To a male, an ovulating female is subconsciously one of the sweetest smells in the world.[35] The scent drives him crazy. (Lap dancers report they earn more on the big "O" days.[36]) So wash off the perfume before slipping into bed with him.

Gentlemen, she will be more turned on by burying her nose in your (somewhat recently washed) armpits than by a coating of your favorite aftershave. Let your natural aroma sexually stimulate her.

Huntresses on the Pill, Read This Carefully

The infamous stink study had opposite results for women on birth control pills. They were more attracted to guys who smelled *similar* to them.[37] Why? It's because the pill simulates the scent of pregnancy. Here's how Mother Nature sees it: "If you're already pregnant, Miss, it's meaningless for you to be with a guy who turns you on. It's better for you to be around people who smell like you, your blood relatives, to help you raise Junior.

"Besides, if you still want sex with the father of your child all the time, it could keep him from going out and impregnating another woman to give me another earthling." Mother Nature stops at nothing!

Bottom line, girl, do not select the lucky man to be your permanent partner and father your children while on the pill. You don't want to wake up next to him someday when you're off it and think, "Ugh, this guy stinks!" Wait to see who smells right when you're off the pregnancy-simulating tablet.

Let's say that, with your Quarry, it's "So far, so good." So very, *very* good. Each date leaves you breathlessly awaiting the next. Sex is spectacular, and you want to stay together under the covers ordering room service for three days straight. Mother Nature is ecstatic because her chemicals are working. Early in the game dopamine is the captain deliriously dancing on the bridge of the Love Boat. Testosterone and estrogen are euphorically singing at the helm. It seems you are right on course toward Happily-Ever-After Land. But if you don't keep a careful eye on the compass, the confused trio can steer you into stormy waters. With just a little more knowledge, however, you can control the deeper love Chemicals and keep the Love Boat afloat forever.

CHAPTER *8*

How to Spark Chemistry for a Relationship

You've been dating for almost a year now. It's fabulous fun, and the sex is mind blowing. You feel miserable when you're apart, and it's magic when you're together. Maybe he's "the one." Perhaps she's the woman you could love forever. You're starting to feel serious—seriously wonderful!

Well, most of the time. Huntresses, you worry because at times he closes off for no reason and won't even tell you what he's thinking. Hunters, you fell for her hard and fast and truly do love her—but you begin to wonder because sometimes she gets overly emotional over "absolutely nothing." He gets angry or she gets pissy, and you both begin to fear your potential permanent Love Partner might become just a brief affair.

The biggest reason dating couples break up is not big fights. It's not infidelity. It's not even mistrust. It's gradually growing disappointment and irritation with each other. That's a pity because you could be perfect for each other in the important things in life: your beliefs, values, goals, and interests. But too often one person starts to find the other aggravating and throws in the towel on a potentially near-perfect relationship.

Why is that so common? Because people don't understand that they're practically dealing with a chemically and neuroanatomically different species! Books have tried to teach us what to do and what to say as well as to speak the other's language. But that's not enough. You must learn how to *think* in a different world—the other sex's brain.

Mars and Venus Told You the *What*, Now the *Why*

Many if not most relationship problems have deep roots in differences between the sexes. But you've known about those for decades. About twenty years ago the author John Gray cleverly and charmingly introduced the world to the non-astrological sense of the planets, Mars and Venus.[1] Back then, readers took copious notes on the challenges that Mr. Mars and Ms. Venus faced with each other:

Mars hides his feelings.	Venus wants to share them.
Mars doesn't listen.	Venus talks more.
Mars quickly offers solutions.	Venus gives unsolicited advice.
Mars wants to feel needed.	Venus needs to feel loved.
Mars reacts with anger.	Venus reacts with emotion and tears.

Nothing has changed in the years since the book *Men Are from Mars, Women Are from Venus* was published. Males still hide feelings, don't listen, quickly offer solutions, want to be needed, and react with anger. Females still share feelings, talk more, give unsolicited advice, need to feel cherished, and react with emotion and tears. It isn't going to change in our lifetime. We are born that way.

For those of you who find gender differences as fascinating as I do, here's more: In preschool a little guy played more competitive games, got angry quicker and more often, fought more, talked later and less, didn't enthusiastically welcome other kids into his games, used more play space, was less sensitive to his friends' feelings, was more interested in objects than people, averaged thirty-six seconds for family goodbyes, identified with the hero or robber in stories, and played with trucks and action toys. If someone did force him to play with dolls, he used them as dive bombers.[2]

Conversely, female tots played fewer competitive games, got angry more slowly and less often, fought less, talked earlier and more, welcomed other kids into their games, were more sensitive to their friends' feelings, used less play space, were more interested in people than objects, averaged ninety-three seconds for family goodbyes, identified with the victim in stories, and played with dolls—not as dive bombers.[3]

Have we changed that much? Neuroscientist Dr. Rhawn Joseph wrote,

> *Within the core of each of us is the child we once were. This child constitutes the foundation of what we have become, who we are, and what we will be.*[4]

So why, these many years after Mars and Venus enlightened our planet, do half of all marriages still end in divorce? John Gray did a great job telling us how to change our behavior, but unfortunately, at that time he didn't have access to the neurological research because it didn't yet exist.

There is a big difference between knowing something and *really* knowing it. You know that a car stalls, but unless you understand the construction under the hood, you can't fix it. Unless you know what chemicals to put in the gas tank, it's not going to stay purring very long. Likewise, unless you know the neuroanatomy, neuro-chemistry, and neuropsychology behind why Mars and Venus are so different, you won't remember what to say when she accuses you of "what" or he does "that." Memorizing phrases isn't enough, and it makes avoiding the same mistakes almost impossible.

When you were a kid you knew you shouldn't lick a frozen flag-pole because your mother told you not to. But you don't really "get it" until you know why: The moisture on your tongue freezes in-stantly, forming an ice bond between your porous, now very painful body part and the pole. Of course you'll have plenty of time to pon-der thermal conductivity while you await the rescue squad. But by then it's too late.

In many ways, in addition to technologically, a kid is smarter than his elders. Once he's felt like a thousand tweezers are ripping off his taste buds, he'll never lick the pole again—no matter how much his big brother double-dog dares him.

Adults, however, don't learn from their lessons. They marry and, not grasping the immense biological/neurological difference—and evolutionary influence—of their mate's brain, get stuck. The ripping away is excruciatingly painful. And then they go out and get stuck all over again. Once again, with a new partner, they vow to stay together—"for richer, for poorer, in sickness or in health, to love and to cherish until death do us part." For far too many couples, unfor-tunately, it's "until misunderstanding, jealousy, or 'I just don't love you anymore' do us part."

Some fortunate few have the ability to swim through the synapses, figuratively speaking, of their Love Partner's brain. The other 99 percent of us need a life preserver to avoid drowning in the foreign rivers.

The Ball of Yarn vs. the Stack of Boxes

Just last week Giorgio and I were sitting on the couch looking at movie listings and had decided on the latest Tom Hanks film. As we were considering the earlier or later show, I asked, "Giorgio, did you know that Tom Hanks is a grandfather?"

Giorgio looked at me quizzically and asked, "What? What's that got to do with whether we go to the six or eight o'clock show?"

"Nothing." I mumbled, "I just thought I'd mention it."

A year ago his response would have exasperated me. But this time, finishing up this book, I caught myself.

I just kissed him on the cheek and said, "Giorgio, you are being so . . . guy."

"Would you want me to be anything else?" he chuckled.

I picked his arm up off the back of the couch and put it around me. "No," I purred.

He kissed my cheek, and we went back to looking at the listings.

Then I asked, "Giorgio, don't you think it's interesting that Hanks is still a big sex symbol and he's a grandfather? How many grandmothers do you think are sex symbols?"

At that, he abruptly stood up to do something in the other room. Oops, I realized. Once again I'd slipped again into "female brain" type of thinking. If I'd been talking with a girlfriend, it would have been perfectly logical for us to go from the movie times . . . to Tom Hanks the actor . . . to Tom Hanks the grandfather . . . to a male sex symbol's age . . . to joking about sex symbol grandmothers. That could even lead to discussing how my grandmother used to cook with a pressure cooker. So you see, it makes perfect sense that we could be talking about movie times one minute and pressure cookers the next. Any woman would understand that. But not Giorgio, not your brother, not your father, not your Quarry, nor your male Love Partner.

His Box Brain

Huntresses, think of a big box with lots of little boxes inside it. That's your man's brain compared to yours. Those interior squares aren't stacked tightly together. In fact, the perimeter of one box doesn't even touch the next. Your man may not neatly fold all his socks and place them in his drawers, but he neatly tucks all his thoughts into separate boxes in his brain like the little boys at my birthday party did with the waffle syrups.

In order to think quickly about another subject that women call "related," he must make the comparatively long voyage across his wide synaptic rivers between neurons. Then he needs time to choose which box the thought should jump into. So when you swim quickly and smoothly from one subject to the next, he thinks you're scattered. And you're infuriated that he can't just casually discuss anything with you.

Girl, be grateful he can compartmentalize like this. Men have the ability to concentrate and focus intently on one problem at a time better because all his thoughts on that matter are squished into one little box.[5] He wants to stay right there until he figures it out and resists if you try to drag him out of it. Giorgio's box brain was still debating the early versus the late show. And a "totally irrational female" was babbling about grandmothers not being sex symbols.

♀ Chemistry Sparker #55

Tell Him If You're Switching Boxes

Huntresses, when you're talking with your PLP and you want to say something you think is related to the subject, he might not see the association. Remember, a male's neurons are more sparsely packed, and this slows down his neural connections. His six and a half times more unmyelinated gray matter further detracts from the speed. So explain the connection to him before saying anything he could possibly think is irrelevant. If he seems confused or exasperated, wind up your point quickly by saying, verbatim, "The bottom line is . . . "

Her Yarn-Ball Brain

Conversely, Hunters, her brain is not a set of organized containers. Think of it as a ball of yarn. Any knitter knows that to form the yarn for storage, you start with a loop, and then wrap the next string around the center of that. As it begins forming a ball, you gradually rotate it until the pieces of yarn are in place. Each string goes in a slightly different direction, but they're much more interconnected than your boxes. Her more closely knit neurons means she can jump effortlessly from one subject to the next, and you might not understand the association. The sudden switch makes some men think it's "screwy thinking."

Don't let it drive you up the wall. Try to grasp the connection of the new topic to what you're discussing. If you can't, just have faith that, in her brain, it *is* relevant. The lady's intricate maze of millions of closely connected neurons can tweet messages all over her brain a thousand times quicker than a lizard's tongue. Gentlemen, you'll find this an advantage for you in some cases!

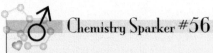

Chemistry Sparker #56

Understand Her Ball of Yarn

Hunters, your lady love has ten times more of that speedy white matter, so of course her thoughts are on fast forward. To your more logical mind, her comment sounds like it's coming out of the blue. The next time she confuses you with something that seems irrelevant, either try to figure out the connection or just smile, shrug, and think, "That's my girl."

P.S. for Huntresses

You might want to try compartmentalizing some of your thoughts in boxes too. It not only helps you get along with your Love Partner better, but it can also keep you from being ticked off at a lot of things. A couple months ago understanding the Stacked Boxes vs. Yarn Ball Concept helped my life in two small ways. It not only saved me from being ticked at Giorgio, but it also got me some lovely lingerie I wouldn't have had.

He had foolishly made the mistake of going shopping with me and was waiting in the safety area near the lingerie department where embarrassed, bored, impatient husbands hang out. As I laid a bra I wanted to buy on the counter, I told the saleswoman I liked it so much that I was going to quickly grab the panties to match. When I returned seconds later, three ladies were in line. I stood on the side, naturally expecting the saleswoman to take me next because I'd been there first. In spite of my strident throat clearing, she continued to ignore me and wait on the others. I was furious and went storming over to Giorgio with a disgusted, "Let's go!"

"Why?" he asked.

"Because I don't want to buy anything from that bitch!" I sputtered, "I was in line and just went away a few seconds to get something else. In the meantime she starts waiting on all those people who hadn't even been in line, without even a smile or apology to me!"

"What's that got to do with the underwear. Do you want to buy it?" he asked.

"Yes!" I almost shouted. "But . . ."

"So?" he interrupted. "The other customers were ready to buy before you were." I started to blow up at him but, thanks to my new insights, I understood. For him, the lingerie was in one mental box, and my fury at the salesperson in another. He saw the two facts as separate, whereas I saw them all intertwined.

I harrumphed, went back, scooped up my purchases and joined the line, realizing he was right. Thanks, Giorgio.

What Are You Thinking About?

Huntresses, put your left hand on the Bible and raise your right in the air. Now try to tell me you've never had this conversation with your Quarry.

You: What are you thinking?

Him: Nothing.

You: Oh, come on. Tell me.

Him: Really, nothing.

You: What do you mean? You've got to be thinking about something.

Him: No, really!

He's telling the truth, Huntresses! Not thinking about something is inconceivable to us. We can never quit because our brain neighborhoods are constantly communicating—on a ground line, no static. His, however, have long periods of silence. When there's nothing specific in one of his boxes to solve, his entire stock of thoughts drains out. His boxes can be completely empty. Nothing in them. Nada. Zip. Zilch.

As a relationship ripens, I've heard many women complain, "He and I have nothing to talk about anymore." But have you ever heard a male groan, "My wife and I can no longer find anything to talk about?" He doesn't care because, for him, silence can spell togetherness.[6]

It is said that one evening the poet William Wordsworth visited his good friend Samuel Taylor Coleridge. The two gentlemen sat silently by the fireside, contentedly smoking their pipes and saying nary a word. As the hours wore on, Mr. Wordsworth stood up, shook his friend's hand, and said, "It has indeed been a delightful evening, Mr. Coleridge."

"The pleasure is all mine," Coleridge replied. And they both meant it!

Can you imagine two girlfriends spending an evening together like that? Males enjoy sitting silently together and just chilling. Giorgio is one of those "strong silent types," and I used to rack my brain for things for us to chat about when we were together. I felt we had to keep talking in order to be communicating.

My new neurological insight has been a real relationship booster for us. Now Giorgio and I sometimes go through an entire dinner with little casual chatting. I can tell that he's much happier in one of his boxes, and I am learning to enjoy my own yarn ball of thoughts sitting silently with him.

Chemistry Sparker #57

Don't Bust into His Boxes

Don't ask your PLP what he's thinking about. When a Hunter is stressed out, retreating and curling up in his cozy "nothing box" is a very comforting place for him to be, and he gets exasperated if you try to yank him out. No matter how much he adores you, he sometimes prefers chilling out alone to chatting. It's crashing his private party to ask, "What are you thinking?" When he emerges, he'll feel closer than if you'd invaded.

How Do You Feel About That?

That's the sequel to the perpetual male query, "What does a woman really want?" The stack of books in my basement oozes with ridiculous advice on "how to get a man to share his feelings." Here are some of the worst suggestions I've read. (To avoid embarrassing the authors, some with recognizable names, I won't reference them.) They recommend telling him:

1) "Honey, I know the male role requires that you be tough, objective, and unemotional. But you'll be even more of a man in my eyes if you can open up to me."
2) "It's okay to have feelings. It's not a sign of weakness."
3) "I don't suspect you're hiding anything from me."
4) "I've always shared my feelings with you. Now all I'm asking is the same."
5) Share your feelings with him honestly first. Then tell him, "See, it wasn't so hard. Now it's your turn."

The ubiquitous, all-time worst advice in those books was "Be sure to look him directly in the eyes when probing his feelings." Males definitely do *not* communicate best gazing into another set of human eyeballs. They'd prefer to be staring down the barrel of a semi-automatic twelve-gauge shotgun. In fact, the deepest guy communication is done sitting side by side in a foxhole, pointing their guns at the same enemy.

Huntresses, what if he insisted that you do something you were physically incapable of doing—like picking him up and hoisting him over your head? Do you think you'd be able to do that if he told you any of the following?

1) "Honey, I know the female role requires that you be soft, feminine, and not muscular. But you'll be more of a woman in my eyes if you hoist me up over your head."
2) "It's okay lifting me up. It's not a sign of being too strong."
3) "I don't suspect you're hiding your physical strength from me."
4) "I've always lifted you up. Now all I'm asking is the same."
5) Hoist her up. Then say, "See, it wasn't so hard. Now it's your turn."

Why He's Tongue-Tied

As I explained in the Introduction, language is housed in the left hemisphere of the brain, and emotions are in the right. Both male and female brains are divided right smack down the middle by a hedge of twenty million nerve fibers called the *corpus callosum*. But that division has a vastly different neuron density for you and your Quarry.[7]

A Hunter's barrier between language and emotions is the Wall of China compared to a Huntress's picket fence. While speaking from his language hemisphere, he has a heck of a time tapping into his emotions on the other side of the great wall. A Huntress hops back and forth over the barrier like a jump rope.

So don't ask your PLP to expound on how he feels. It's not that he doesn't want to talk about his feelings. He can't and, because the average guy doesn't like to admit he's incapable of anything, he gets annoyed. So sisters, if you decide to stay heterosexual, don't expect much discussion of feelings with your partner. If, however, getting your man's feelings on something is of life-and-death importance to you, here's a tip on how to do it.

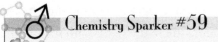

Chemistry Sparker #58

Give Your Questions a Corporate Spin

Choose a time when he's not expected to do any deep gazing into your eyes. Then substitute more corporate phrases like, "What is your take on that?" "Let me run a few questions past you," or "What's your appraisal of the situation?" (Never ever use the word *feel*.) And, heaven forbid, don't ever, ever preface it with "We need to talk."

Hunters, it's the opposite for a woman. Asking her feelings is a mammoth togetherness booster.

Chemistry Sparker #59

Ask Her "How Do You Feel About That?"

Hunters, the next time you and your Quarry are chatting about anything, anytime, anywhere, that anyone could possibly have any emotions about—good or bad—gaze into her eyes and soulfully ask, "How do you *feel* about that?" After you pick her up off the floor and revive her with smelling salts, she'll swoon with feelings of closeness.

Learn a Very Different Body Language

Gentlemen, as tough as it is to express your feelings, it's tougher for you to recognize hers. If you put observation of your Love Partner's teary eyes in one box, her quivering lips in another, and her hanging head in another, how could you possibly be expected to connect the dots and determine she's upset? Besides, you've been brought up to believe that letting your emotions show is a sign of weakness. So you're probably assuming, "I'm sure she wouldn't want me to notice."

I'd like to help you change your thinking. Consider the usefulness of reading emotions. I'll put it in guy terms. There you are at the poker table. The lights are low and the smoke is thick. You stare over the mountain of chips at the guy across from you. It's just you and him now. You've got a sweet straight in your hand, but the dude just keeps raising the stakes. His expression is placid and his eyes are drilling a hole into your face. What's going on? Is he bluffing?

You take a chance. You call and lay down your cards.

YES! The pot is yours.

How did you outsmart your opponent? You had developed the talent to read micro-expressions. It wasn't obvious. Your adversary hadn't sucked in his breath or glanced away even for a flash. But when he raised his eyebrows and pulled them together for a fraction of a second, you sensed it was sheer fear. You smelled it as clear as cow dung.

The biggest winners in business and sports are expert readers of emotions. A world-class chess player senses how firmly his opponent holds his piece and how quickly he places it. Your enemy's face and body telegraph his strategy, training, determination—but only if you know how to read him. So get out there, dude, and master the skill of reading micro-expressions. You just need a little practice. How?

Grit your teeth and hang in there with me on this next suggestion. Step one: Download a daytime soap opera and watch it with the sound off. You'll see the whole gamut of emotions—anger, acceptance, anticipation, aversion, sadness, surprise, and hundreds in between. See how many you can name in the silent show.

Step two: Now turn the sound on and suffer through it again. On average, a Huntress would recognize eighteen out of twenty emotions correctly.[8] A guy's doing well if he can identify five.

Now watch it yet again with the sound off and practice, practice, practice. You'll get the hang of reading emotions soon.

Former Army psychologist Paul Ekman, one of *Time* magazine's world's one hundred most influential people in 2009, trains police interrogators and authorities in the art and science of face reading. Now he's developed a program to detect whether a couple is headed for the divorce court from just fifteen seconds of watching their interaction.[9] Their flashes of indifference to each other's subtle feelings play a big role. To keep the Sparks flying, try to adjust your antennae to pick up her subtle expressions.

Chemistry Sparker #60

Detect Her Micro-Expressions

Hunters, being sensitive to your Quarry's feelings is a biggie in making your Chemistry last. Practice the talent, and when you detect she's upset, ask her what's wrong. Then *listen*, nod. *Listen*, sympathize. *Listen*, comfort her. But do not offer solutions—until she asks.

Guys, there's another reason to acknowledge her emotions: If you don't, she'll get angry and start arguing with you. And due to her brain's more direct connection between emotions and language, you'll probably lose!

Shall We Talk It Out, or Slug It Out?

I'll never forget a totally confounding (at the time) experience I had in Seattle. A client who had booked me for a seminar picked me up at the airport. On the way to the hotel, Bernard briefed me about the group, the room setup, the AV arrangements, and he gave me my handouts he'd printed. Suddenly a Honda in front of us came to a screeching halt, just missing what could have been a major fender bender. I turned toward Bernard to tell him how lucky it was that he saw the car and stopped, but he was already shaking a furious fist at the other car. The other driver bellowed, "I had to stop, you idiot, or I would have hit the car in front of me."

"You could have gotten us killed you sonnuva-bitch," Bernard bellowed. That was met with a hand darting out of the Honda's window, middle finger raised in the air—the inner-city sign of war. Figuring the finger wasn't Hulk Hogan's or Mike Tyson's, Bernard leapt out of the car. All I saw was a flurry of flushed faces and flailing arms. Finally he stormed back, but not before banging his fist on the finger giver's car. Why did he react so physically? Because a male's limbic system is more wired to the physical than the linguistic.[10]

"Asshole!" he bellowed. I thought, but of course didn't say, "Asshole" had a point. He did have to stop suddenly to avoid hitting the next car. Grumbling, Bernard got back into the car, where I was pretending to go over the handouts.

I lost something in his car that day: my respect for Bernard. If he had been my boyfriend, brother, or husband, I would have been furious and spent the rest of the ride trying to explain to him why the other guy was right. A.H. did indeed need to stop suddenly. If I'd known then what I know now, however, I would have considered Bernard's blowup just a rude male burp. His emotions, fueled by testosterone, shot straight to his biceps, bypassing any rational thought.

The rest of the time in Seattle, Bernard was an ideal client. Unfortunately, due to his irrational blowup, I was unable to give him the respect he deserved and the gratitude I wish I'd expressed.

Huntresses, your man didn't exactly come out of the womb baring his toothlessness or clenching his tiny fists. But the anger and aggression circuits were already formed by the time he let out his first yelp.[11] When the doctor held him upside-down by his tiny pink feet and spanked his bottom, the newborn dude probably wanted to kill him. While kindergarten guys were slugging it out in the playground over a dispute, we were talking out our differences in the sandbox.

And of course, evolution gets into the act. If, instead of facing the small-fingered Honda driver, a Cro-Magnon Bernard found himself staring into the eyes of a livid lioness, what was he supposed to do? Say "Down puddy cat," or "Let's talk about this"? No, he pulls out his homemade ax or hurls his hunga munga. The womenfolk back in the cave are delighted. And he is delighted when they don't scold him for his angry reaction.

There's more. Don't forget his childhood, the acculturated "show 'em how tough you are, kid" influence. Let's put this into Cognitive Science language: "Limbic (emotional) activation in the female brain is linked to verbal response areas," and "Limbic activation in the male brain is linked to motor/physical response areas."[12] In a sense, his anger chemicals go straight to his fists, hers to her tongue. When he's furious, his amygdala says "Pull the trigger." Hers says, "Tell one of your girlfriends."

✚ Chemistry Sparker #61

Don't Talk When He's Fuming

Huntresses, between his limbic system being wired to the physical rather than the linguistic, plus evolution, plus his upbringing, plus ten times more testosterone, what do you expect?

Ignore and forgive your Quarry's outbursts. It's anatomy, evolution, and upbringing all rolled up into one "anger ball," and it will pass.

Hunters, your advice is just the opposite. Ask her to tell you all about the problem, every minute detail. If you have the misfortune of being the one she's pissed at, just listen quietly and then repeat one or more of the following phrases:

"I'm sorry I [fill in what she's accusing of you of]."

"You're absolutely right. I had no right to [fill in what she's accusing of you of]."

"I can't believe I was so thoughtless to [fill in what she's accusing of you of]."

"Can you ever forgive me for [fill in what she's accusing of you of]?"

"I promise [fill in what she's accusing of you of] will never happen again."

Then, as soon as she's calmed down, hug her and tell her you love her.

See how easy that was?

⚧ Chemistry Sparker #62

Grill Her for the Details

When your Quarry is angry, Hunters, don't turn away. Soften your body language, look her directly in the eyes, and ask all the ins and outs of what's bothering her. Her emotions are more tied to the linguistic, so unlike you, she'll love talking it out. Nod often and toss in an occasional "I understand." Then use a selection of the above phrases liberally and finish her off with a hug. Don't fight fire with fire. Snuff it out with the bonding chemical, oxytocin.

Congratulations to both of you. The two of you have done everything right so far. Huntresses, you Sparked your Quarry with sexual bait and reeled him in with your fine qualities. Hunters, you Sparked hers by showing that you're husband material right up front. You both collaborated with Mother Nature to enhance the passion. You used neuroanatomical and chemical insights into your Quarry's box- or ball of yarn–type brain to navigate the Love Boat away from the jagged rocks. You're ecstatically happy and tell everyone you are "in love." But now let's learn how to Spark the Chemistry to make it the real thing, the kind of true love that makes your Quarry crave lasting togetherness with you.

CHAPTER *9*

How to Spark Chemistry for Falling in Love

You're in love . . . life is superb . . . your heart explodes with joy and everybody notices. You're always laughing and smiling and sometimes you burst into song. The world is brighter and more beautiful than ever, even on rainy days. Things that used to bother you, like traffic, annoying colleagues, and toilet tissue rolling from underneath instead of over the top, just make you smile. Nothing matters except being with your loved one. This exhilarating and electrifying stage of love consumes you. Your *Pleasure Island* is deluged by dopamine, and it is sheer ecstasy. Enjoy every euphoric moment of it!

Fortunately, you now realize that love, in the song and sonnet sense, is a chemical assault on your brain, albeit a fabulous one. This knowledge can help you make the best choice of your life—or save yourself from making a grave mistake. Before taking the big step, I suggest you run a few final tests on your Potential Love Partner. Squint and search beyond the glittering stars in your eyes to ensure that your love will last and last and last. And prove to your Potential Love Partner that you have the lasting qualities too.

Clear vision is tough when dopamine is hacking the texts between your amygdala and your prefrontal cortex. It's not that the *Professor* hasn't been trying to warn you if he happens to feel this particular partner isn't right for you. He's been frantically tweeting all the other brain regions that trouble could be lurking behind the altar. But Mother Nature shushes him by shooting you up with more dopamine to make you even crazier for your Quarry. But all this drama is exciting, like a frightening film, and you can mistake it for true love. Here's how to tell if it really is—and to show your PLP that you have the character and the qualities that make you "the one." To do this, employ what I call the "Big Four." Each is based on the latest studies of what both sexes seek in a permanent partner.

Is This Quarry a Keeper?

Concentrate on clearing the paths between the emotional and rational parts of your brain. I'm not just speaking figuratively. You now understand how the love druggies ambush the messages so you're literally "crazy in love." If you still love, respect, and feel wonderful about him—and yourself—after about a year and a half, don't let this one get away. You've found a keeper! It's only when you feel "sanely" in love with her and not "crazy" in love that can you take back the controls of the Love Boat.

Why Is He Afraid to Commit?

Huntresses, how many times have you heard that? A hundred? Two hundred? But you may not have heard this answer. No offense insinuated, but it's probably because when a smart guy gets serious, he gets smarter—*almost* as smart as you've been all along! I find it interesting that men fall in love more often than women.[1] But then they're more apt to balk. Why? Because if the relationship gets serious, men too become sensitive, consciously or subconsciously, to substantial qualities in their Potential Love Partner. They just take longer to come around to it.

During the electrifying initial dating stages he doesn't analyze stuff to death. A guy-type brain doesn't consciously conjecture, "What is her relationship with her mother and what does it signify?" He's not going to sit down with a beer and a buddy and ask, "Hey, dude, how much do you think she's going to help me realize my aspirations?" or "Do you think she's still going to enjoy cave spelunking with me a year from now?" However, when a male finds himself contemplating the long term, he gets a hazy sense of these things. That's why sometimes everything can be going great in your relationship. The two of you seem to be running full-speed ahead toward total togetherness, even the altar. Then, just before you get there, *screech!* He slams on the brakes.

Many women would say, "He got cold feet," or "He's commitment-phobic." It's more likely that it finally got through to his dopamine/testosterone-marinated skull that he and his girlfriend were not a fit in some of the more important matters in life. To demonstrate that you are the one for him, you must find subtle ways to hint to your Quarry that you are a match for the "Big Four."

1) Do you and your Potential Love Partner have similar deep beliefs and values in life?
2) Do your definitions of "togetherness" match?
3) Can your Potential Love Partner be depended on if adversity strikes?
4) Will you each encourage your partner's personal and professional growth?

While manifesting (not misrepresenting!) certain attributes, also keep a checklist on your PLP. Without certain components and similarities between you, long-lasting Chemistry is almost impossible. Your differences will chomp away at your love, bite by bite, until your plate is empty—and you're both starving for love with someone else.

Let's talk about the Big Four in order.

I See Life That Way Too!

Which statement expresses what you want in a life partner?

A. *I want someone different from me.* Someone exciting who has a fascinating lifestyle, exposes me to new ideas, gives me fresh insights, shares adventures, and helps me view the world in a different way.

B. *I want someone similar to me.* Someone who is in accord with my deep beliefs and principles, makes me feel secure, enjoys similar activities, likes my lifestyle, and understands how I look at life.

Of course, your answer is "both." Everyone wants someone similar in some of life's most important ways and different in the fun frills.[2] We crave excitement, ecstasy, thrills, and chills. We also long for serenity, commitment, contentment, and comfort.

Think back to the days when you were in school. Remember how there were various cliques? The preppies? The tough gang? The brains? The athletes? The self-proclaimed cool kids? Chances are that there weren't too many cross-friendships because people feel comfortable with their own.

While moving into a college dormitory, college students were interviewed about their beliefs, values, ethics, mores, and morals. Researchers hypothesized that, as the students got to know each other, the ones who looked at life in the same way would gravitate toward each other.[3] Sure enough, they hardly missed a beat. Cliques of similar kids formed.

Your prefrontal cortex, the wise brainy *Professor,* knows that if a relationship is going to work, you need a mate who looks at life in the same way as you. Let's face it—life is confusing and scary. TV, magazines, newspapers, millions of blogs, and social media—and all other methods of communication now known or currently being developed—can make your head spin. When you find another human being who has come to the same conclusions about life, you feel protected and out of harm's way. Your opinions, morals, beliefs, and values are vindicated by your Love Partner's agreement. This floods your brain with oxytocin, the attachment chemical.

Obviously your agreement is not necessary or even desired on everything. That would be boring. What matters is not the number of agreements on small things but rather harmony on the more weighty matters in life that causes "coupling," as researchers call it.[4]

Agreement on certain subtleties in life is often more important to females. Hunters, if you've pretended to share her dedication to animal rights, care for the elderly, and protecting the environment, how do you think she'll feel when you kick her cat, ignore your grandmother, or refuse to recycle?

Men don't need agreement as much as they need respect that their choices are good.[5] I'll never forget an episode in the then-popular TV show, *House.* The characters were musing about how much they valued their parents' love. Dr. Gregory House groused,

"All I wanted was for my father to say I was *right*." It confused me at the time, but now, after gaining a better understanding of the neuropsychology of the male brain, it makes perfect sense.

Huntresses, if he's a vegetarian or macrobiotic, it doesn't mean you have to slurp seaweed soup with him every night. Just show your support for his preference. Tell him he's smart to make such a disciplined and wise choice.

♀♂ Chemistry Sparker #63

Show You Share or Respect Your Quarry's Values

To stoke the fire in your relationship, find ways to highlight your similarities whenever you can. Emphasize your admiration for your PLP's beliefs.

Hunters, when you feel the same way about things she deeply cares about, oxytocin floods her brain. Huntresses, confirming his commitments and supporting his principles has the same effect on him.

But express the similarity only if it's true! Otherwise you're steering the Love Boat in a deadly direction, and your relationship goes aground. If it is going to stay afloat beyond the crazy dopamine-drenched days of early love, similar principles and convictions are must haves.

But that's not the whole picture. Three other major pieces must fit in the successful relationship puzzle.

How Do You Define "Togetherness"?

How close do you want to be to your partner? Together every day, every night? Inseparable? Having the same friends and interests as he does? Doing the same activities with her? Or is "togetherness" cohabitation, companionship? Living under the same roof, in the same bed, but coming and going as you please? You spending time with your friends and he with his? You going wherever you like, pursuing your passions, and she hers? In short, how would you define "togetherness?"

Togetherness can mean one or the other of the above—or something in between. The definition must be the same for both of you, or else the sticky wicket can shatter the bonding Chemistry.[6] Finding out your PLP's views can be a tricky task, especially for women. Asking outright could make him feel like he's being water-boarded, so listen between the lines. What does he say about his parent's relationship? His friends? Does he joke about a buddy "getting hooked," "biting the dust," "putting on the ball and chain"? Or does he use words more like his buddy "is hearing the ol' wedding bells," "decided to settle down," or "found the right one"?

Guys, what about her? Does she ever talk about any of her past boyfriends "suffocating her," "being too possessive," or "never letting her out of his sight"? Conversely, perhaps she complains about a previous boyfriend "not being with her enough" or that he was "always running around with his buddies." Does she bemoan the fact that her father was never home?

What about family feelings? How often does he talk to his mom? His dad? Are they close? Does she spend holidays with her family? Does he speak with his siblings, aunts, uncles, cousins, and other various and sundry relatives? If he hasn't been a bonder in his previous life, do you think he'll have a frontal lobotomy and start loving family life now? Psych it out and compare it to your togetherness quotient.

Researchers call how you "score" on the togetherness chart your "comparison level," and it plays a big part in keeping the love Chemistry between you.[7] "I thought he would change" are some of the most foolish words I've ever heard.

My cousin Rory and his wife, Camilla, whom I knew way before they got married, have two beautiful young daughters, but they're going through a tough time this year. Rory has always had vast interests and continually finds new hobbies. He had a meditation phase, a bird-watching phase, and a bowling phase. Now he's into calligraphy and going to comic book conventions.

A few months ago Camilla and I curled up on the couch with our coffee cups and had a poignant talk. She was lamenting that Rory was always off with his friends. I squeezed her hand and reminded her, "Rory has a lot of diverse interests. Before you were married, I remember you telling me how fascinating he was because of it."

"I know, Leil, but I thought that when the girls came along, he would settle down."

"Camilla, what do you most enjoy doing?" I asked her.

"Just being with my girls. I mean that's really my favorite thing to do. It's just that . . . well, I feel Rory should be here more. The family should be doing things together."

Here's the tragedy. This very weekend Rory and Camilla are planning to tell their girls they are splitting. My eyes water as I write this. If only Rory and Camilla had discovered they had totally different definitions of "togetherness." For Camilla, it is constant closeness.

For Rory, it is loving cohabitation. Who will suffer the most from their not scoping it out before? Their girls, of course.

The so-called logical advice here would be to "sit down now and talk about how you both define togetherness." Sounds good, but unfortunately that's not always realistic. Most Hunters are biologically challenged in illusive relationship discussions like that. It's like asking a mermaid to do the splits. And a Huntress's crystal ball is too chemically clouded during early passionate love to think straight.

The solution? Make an appointment for your wise *Professor* and emotional amygdala to have a little non-dopamine-hacked neurotransmitting about what a relationship means to you.

☿♂ Chemistry Sparker #64

Emphasize Your Similar Concept of Togetherness

Make it a point to define clearly and consciously what "togetherness" means to you. Then, to the best of your ability, determine what it means to your Potential Love Partner. If, hopefully, you discover that you and your PLP's are the same, find ways to underscore it in casual conversation.

And remember (especially Huntresses), if you're thinking, "I can change him," forget about it. If you succeed, call the *Guinness Book of World Records.*

"In Sickness and in Health"

To me, those words are the most moving most part of a wedding ceremony because I've seen how illness and adversity affects couples.

After deep love has had time to take root, tragedy can draw a couple even closer together. Whether they have taken the actual marriage vows or not, taking care of a long-term Love Partner can intensify love and make it more enduring.[8]

Infirmity and adversity have the power to overshadow other problems that start to tear a couple apart. In many cases, when there are catastrophic challenges, major arguments vanish and money problems pale. "You left the cap off the toothpaste" and "Take out the garbage" are no longer declarations of war. In fact, those minor foibles can invoke smiles reminiscent of early posthoneymoon discoveries.

I've seen it happen twice, once due to severe injury in a small plane crash and the other Parkinson's disease. Both my friends' marriages were tottering, but when tragedy struck, the other partner went instantly from being a quarreler to a loving caregiver. Life was harder, but their love became stronger.

A few months into writing this book I learned firsthand the bonding effect of illness. I was glued to the keyboard morning to night and had put off a lot of "should do" things like having a mammogram. Giorgio bugged me incessantly about it. So despite my grumbling, he insisted and dragged me off to the hospital.

A week later the hospital "invited" me back for a repeat visit. When I heard my gynecologist's sympathetic "Hello" on the phone a few days later, I realized there'd be a slight change of schedule during the next few months.

Chemo for breast cancer sucked, but I discovered a new closeness with Giorgio. He postponed taking command of the ship he was booked for in Italy, becoming my hospital chauffeur and staying with me during every depressing chemo session. Giorgio spent the months puffing up my pillows, rubbing my nauseous tummy, kissing my yucky red face, caressing my bald head, and lying to me, saying I looked beautiful.

Now I'm completely okay. No, I'm better than okay because it showed me how vital togetherness is. Whether official vows have been exchanged or not, unspoken ones can be just as powerful. After that experience I have a deeper understanding of the distinction between "being in love" and loving. I'm sure the many millions of couples who have had experiences like mine understand what I'm talking about.

So here's a question you should ask yourself when considering exchanging togetherness promises: "If tragedy struck, would my Potential Love Partner be able to take on the role of caregiver?" When you're flat on your back, it's no fun lying there alone. And equally important, "Would I do the same?"

I pray you will never need it, but think about it now because this is the person you plan to spend the rest of your life with in whatever shape either of you is in. Find ways to let your partner know you'll be there, for better or for worse. Here's how.

♀♂ Chemistry Sparker #65

Show Your Quarry That You're a Caregiver

Be extra-attentive and loving when your Quarry isn't feeling well. Giving her flowers when she's sick is as meaningful as on her birthday, maybe more so. Taking him chicken soup when he's flat on his back gives him nurse fantasies of the nonsexual kind—and those last a lot longer.

And of course, check out your Quarry for care-giving qualities. It's bad enough to be sick. But to have no one to hold your hand when you're sick *really* sucks.

The Magnificent Twenty-First-Century Mantra—Personal Growth

I don't need to tell you the twenty-first-century world is practically a different planet. We are inspired by different ideas, connected by diverse technologies, admired for distinct accomplishments, and desired for divergent qualities—some old, some new. How lovely that we live in a land where free expression and diversity are encouraged and where poverty and plagues don't prohibit it as they often did in the past. In many parts of the world personal growth would be considered a luxury just for the rich. For those of us in more fortunate nations it is ubiquitous and adds a thrilling dimension to our lives.

Marriage is no longer the economic and social institution it used to be. The expectations and psychological needs of the partners bear little resemblance to even a hundred years ago. Nora in Ibsen's late-nineteenth-century play *A Doll's House* would be ecstatic knowing that, within a scant fifty years, a group of women calling themselves feminists would lay the cornerstone for the temple of personal growth at which both evolved men and women worship today. Sociologists call it "self-expansion."[9] The more a mate encourages your goals, the happier and more committed your togetherness will be.[10]

In days gone by, happily in the past, it was primarily the woman who was expected to serve her partner. A "dutiful wife" brought hubby his slippers, didn't complain if he worked late, and entertained his colleagues whenever requested. Now it's a two-way street, and women who work just as hard expect and deserve the same deference. Both

Hunters and Huntresses have their antennae out for a Love Partner who will be there for them both personally and professionally.

♀♂ Chemistry Sparker #66

Show Signs That You Can Help Your Quarry Grow

Today you have the luxury of adding personal growth to your wish list and expecting it. Hunters, whenever the subject of her personal and professional goals comes up, tell her how supportive you are. Huntresses, when he speaks of his aspirations, share his enthusiasm and enhance his confidence that he can achieve them.

Before making the Big Decision, however, make sure it works the other way too. Chemistry can die quickly if your own creativity and growth are stifled.

"Vet" Your Quarry

As my regular readers know, I have a huge loft in New York City that, without rent control and a housemate, I could never afford. When I first found it, I was in the habit of having short-term housemates, students or professionals on short assignments in the city, for which I advertised in a then-popular weekly paper.

One of my ads came out on Thursday. On Friday, Keith, a thirty-six-year-old cellist with the Boston Symphony who was recently separated from his wife, called. He came over on Saturday and moved in on Sunday.

Keith was a fabulous housemate, not like the previous one who left the toilet seat up with a vengeance. The only annoyance was the ghastly ringtone on his cell. Several times an evening, Manowar's *Dark Avenger* blasted out on his phone. He'd answer it with an anguished expression and disappear into his room.

I once joked about his ringtone. He shook his head, "I hate it too."

"Well, um, Keith why do you have it?"

"My wife—soon to be EX-wife—insisted."

"Oh, she was into heavy metal?" I asked.

"No!" he blurted out. "She always liked classical. Then one day, right out of the blue, she starts listening to Slayer and Spinal Tap and turns the volume up as high as it will go."

"You mean it was all of a sudden?" I queried.

"Well, not really; bizarre things started happening last year."

"Keith, please don't answer if I'm invading your privacy, but may I ask what?"

He stared at me for a moment, took a deep breath, and said, "Okay, here goes. The first thing I noticed was she'd start talking about something, and I couldn't follow her train of thought. At first I thought it was just me until one time at a dinner party, for no reason, she starts talking about Obi-Wan Kenobi, the *Star Wars* character. The party's host asked who Obi-Wan Kenobi was. My wife breaks out laughing hysterically, and won't stop. Everybody looked at each other, wondering what the heck was going on.

"After that, there was all kinds of other weird stuff."

"Like?"

He put his elbows on the table and his head in his hands. "Jeez, Leil, the whole gambit. First she'd garble about some new age mumbo jumbo. Then she'd babble about a fatal accident if we didn't believe in Biblical miracles. I mean, she took them literally." When he raised his head, I saw his eyes watering. Embarrassed, he stood up. "I dunno. Maybe it runs in the family. Her mom was a bit of a kook too." Just then Manowar's "Dark Avenger" blasted out on his phone. He slammed on the silencer and disappeared into his room.

Keith's story rang a bell. A few friends in the past had told me that they'd known someone who had "suddenly gone sort of nuts." They often followed it by saying they had heard the person's mother or father was "very eccentric" too. Other times I'd hear, "She was abused as a child," or "He was raised by an alcoholic father."

Lovers seldom realize that their potential partner's childhood can have a direct impact on their future relationships and desire for a long-term one.[11] During casual discussions with your PLP try to steer the subject around to his childhood. Did his parents love him? Was there any brutality in his family? Did his mother suffer severe stress while he was still in her womb? Even that could have a detrimental effect on his later psychological development.[12] And yes, it's chemical. Growing up in a loving environment increases oxytocin in his body, meaning he'll be a better bonder.

Hunters, what about her? Did she have a stable upbringing? Did any of her close blood relatives suffer from mental illness? Was she a troubled child? As callous as it sounds, if you intend to raise a family with this lady, it's worth determining if there was any potentially transmittable mental illness or childhood challenge that could surface in adulthood. It's not likely but definitely worth keeping your eyes open for when you start thinking about being together for the rest of your life.

As we discussed, often an affliction can create closeness between loved ones. But tragically, there are some behavioral conditions due to childhood or inherited genetic abnormalities that don't. There's a very good chance it won't ever manifest itself, so don't freak out about this. But it pays to be extra vigilant when considering someone you'll be with for the rest of your life. Don't dismiss clues like Keith did.

This sounds like pretty depressing stuff, doesn't it? So I'm going to just drop it here and beg you to read a document you'll find on the web. Before saying "I do" or giving up your rent-controlled apartment, run a search for the "Surgeon General's Report on the Risk Factors of Certain Mental Conditions, Chapter Three, Section Two." Don't skip the part on "Family and Genetic Factors." The percentage of inheritable and upbringing-influenced conditions is staggering.

Chemistry Sparker #67

Probe Your Chosen PLP's Childhood (and Genes!)

This is what the dating process is all about—figuring whether your future togetherness will be happy or horrible. While having fun together and fantasizing about a beautiful life, don't forget to climb out on the branches of your PLP's family tree to look for nuts. (Sorry, bad pun.) Scamper through your loved one's childhood to sniff out possible future challenges. Also, avoid doing anything irrational that your PLP might mistake as having deeper roots.

Look at it this way: You wouldn't buy an expensive purebred dog without seeing its papers and assuring yourself that it has no inheritable diseases. And you're going to live with your loved one a lot longer than your dog!

May I Have a Word with Young Lovers?

"Life without him would be a life without meaning."

"I'll die if she ever leaves me."

"I could never fall in love with anyone else."

"It is fate we should be together forever."

Have you ever felt this way when you were very young? We all did once or twice. Some thrice. At age seventeen I thought I'd found the love of my life, the boy I just *knew* was the one. He was older and what some would call a tough guy. But he could be oh-so tender! I was ecstatic when he started talking about a future with me. "Our forever together time," he called it.

Butch and I had been dating for about three months, but my mother hadn't met him yet. Instead of coming to the door to pick me up, he would park in front of my house and honk the horn. It was to the tune of "shave-and-a-haircut, two bits," the then-sweetest sound in the world to me. Upon hearing it I'd bounce out the door and breathlessly race to his car for a few hours of blissful together-ness and discussing "our forever together time."

One day my mother asked me, "Leilie, do you have a date with Butch tonight?"

"Yes," I crooned.

"He sounds so nice from what you've told me about him, dear. Why don't you invite him in for a few minutes? I'd love to meet him."

"But Mama . . ."

"Just for a few minutes, dear. I promise."

At the anxiously awaited shave-and-a-haircut-two-bits, I ran out and begged him to come in to say "hi" to her.

After a short, noticeably uncomfortable conversation, my mother asked, "Leilie, can you come into my room for a second?" She closed her door and literally lay down across the doorway. She pointed a furious finger up at me and gave notice: "You will go out with that boy over my dead body!" She stormed back to the living room, locking her door behind her with me inside. I never saw Butch again.

Then, just several months ago, I got a letter written in a typeface I call "nut font" from, I kid you not, a return address of the Maryland Department of Corrections. Apparently, Butch's brother had found me on the web for him. Looking back, I shudder to think of what a nightmare my life would have been if we'd gone through with our "forever together time."

So, Dear Reader, if you haven't reached the big two-oh, don't even think about the "M" word! It's practically impossible to make the right choice at your age. It's not because you're not smart. You could be the brightest crayon in the Crayola factory, but the biological structure of your brain is not prepared to make one of the most important decisions of your life. You don't have to believe Mom or Dad—let neuroscience tell you why.

Don't Marry Until You're Myelinated (Parents, Don't Miss This!)

Until I'm what? No, it wasn't a typo. As you now know, the neurons in your brain are constantly communicating by electrical impulses. The tubular-shaped insulation I mentioned earlier, called a myelin sheath, protects them from hit-and-miss thinking. This sheath, a greased tube of sorts around the axons of your neurons, only develops gradually. When you were born, the myelin in your system was hardly detectable.[13] That's why an as-yet myelinated baby sleeps in a crib. She might sense that falling out of bed would be a big "ouch," but the message emanating from her little prefrontal cortex is too slow. Her tiny little *Professor* doesn't have time to get the message to her central nervous system to stop her from rolling toward the cliff. In your early twenties, when your neurons become more fully myelinated, those greased tubes transmit clearer messages to the rest of your brain faster.[14] (Sorry, young lovers, the full myelination process isn't complete until about age twenty-five.)

I know it feels so intense. Your world revolves around your romance. But if it saves even one of you from ruining your life, I'm going to break my own commitment to not quote tedious excerpts from studies. This is from "Defining the Brain Systems of Lust, Romantic Attraction, and Attachment," published in the *Archives of Sexual Behavior* by five of the leading researchers in the field.[15]

> *We were able to demonstrate that adolescents in early-stage intense romantic love did not differ from patients during a hippomanic stage . . . intense romantic love in teenagers is a "psycho pathologically prominent stage."*

Pathological means "evidencing a mentally disturbed condition."

Okay, throw this book out the window or delete it. But I speak the truth.

Shall We Make a Federal Case Out of It?

In my grandmother's day sex before marriage was a sin. Even in my mother's day, living together before marriage was a couple's guilty secret. In today's rapidly evolved society, however, I think premarital cohabitation should be a must, even a constitutional amendment! Permanent vows should come only after you have passed the test of togetherness, at least a year and a half to be safe. And don't even think about bringing another human being into our already-overpopulated world before then!

Incidentally, if I should mysteriously get struck by lightning before this book is published, you know it was Mother Nature taking careful aim.

CHAPTER 10

How to Spark Chemistry for a Lifetime of Love

Love is the most beautiful of dreams and the worst of nightmares.
—William Shakespeare

At age eighteen this playwright married a lady of twenty-six, fathered a baby six months later, indulged in out-of wedlock sex, left his wife three years later, went on to multiple affairs with younger females, and wrote 126 love poems to a male known only as "Young Lord" or "Fair Youth."[1] Obviously the bard knew a thing or two about the nightmares part!

I far prefer this quotation written by a man who had once been a motorcycle messenger and a mechanic. The insightful author, Louis de Bernières, acknowledged the madness of romance yet understood that only those who wait until the frenzy passes will discover the magic of true love.

Love is a temporary madness. It erupts like volcanoes and then subsides. And when it subsides you have to make a decision. You have to work out whether your roots have become so entwined together that it is inconceivable that you should ever part. Because this is what love is.

Love is not breathlessness, it is not excitement, it is not the promulgation of promises of eternal passion. . . . That is just being "in love" which any fool can do. Love itself is what is left over when "being in love" has burned away, and this is both an art and a fortunate accident. Your mother and I had it, we had roots that grew towards each other underground, and when all the pretty blossoms had fallen from our branches we found that we were one tree and not two.[2]

At the beginning of your relationship, the delirium of discovery and fantasies of the future make the chemicals in your brain gush like a new oil well. You're singing in the rain, dancing between the stars, frolicking on cloud nine. The frenzy is so fantastic that reality doesn't get through to the brighter part of your brain up front. You and your beloved close your eyes to all the signs: "Warning!" "Danger Ahead!" "Proceed with caution!" Early love is definitely not a drug-free zone.

Making Beautiful Beginnings Last Forever

Huntresses, after you're engaged, girlfriends flock around you, oohing and aahing over your ring. Caterers call to tempt you with delicious finger foods that your wedding guests will devour. Bakers entice you with pictures of multitiered white castles with a miniature of you and your lucky man on top. On the big day you will wear the most exquisite dress you'll ever own, and he will look so dashing in his tux.

Hunters, you may be less involved in the preparations for the big day, but you're just as excited. Your buddies tease and slap you on the back. But under their joking put-downs, you know you've got one up on them because you've found the one. And besides, the guys throw you one helluva good bachelor party.

Your family and friends will give you ridiculously costly crystal, kitchen gadgets, and knick-knacks. Then you'll cast off on the real Love Boat, a cruise to the Caribbean to drink Mai Tais on the beach, dance 'til dawn, and indulge in lovemaking that would make rabbits seem celibate.

But the bridal industry has a dirty little secret that wedding magazines and vendors don't tell you. When you come home from the honeymoon, no one makes a fuss over you anymore. No bakers begging, no caterers calling, no friends congratulating. You become just normal folks. At that point you look at each other and think, "Where have all the hours gone? Is it really over? Where's all the excitement?"

Is either of you disappointed in your mate or wish you hadn't taken the big step? Of course not! You still love each other as much as ever and know in your heart you made the right choice. So what's happening? Why is it no longer as exhilarating?

Journalists write about a phenomenon called "postwedding blues." Sociologists say "postnuptial depression."[3] But only Cognitive Science can tell you precisely why you feel this way. Up until the honeymoon cruise ship sailed home, dopamine was gushing like a volcano. Your systems were swimming with serotonin, and both your pleasure centers were as bright as flashing cameras taking beautiful pictures of what was to come.

"Okay, no big deal," you shrug. Life is good, your mate is great, and your love is strong. The small discoveries about your loved one give you a chuckle. The way he scrunches the toothpaste and leaves the cap off is so cute. You smile at the way she "gently hints" you should take out the garbage. Dopamine and serotonin start dancing again.

However, this time it's more of a waltz than a samba. *Pleasure Island* lights up again, but now it's more like a night-light than a spotlight. You settle into a routine. Up at seven, off to work at eight, back home by six, dinner by seven, a few hours in front of a screen, and to bed by eleven.

Sex is still good, but she's put away the beaded penis wrap and mirrors. She doesn't scream as loud, and he's down from an hour of foreplay to ten minutes. And then there's her occasional headache. You no longer crave his company every minute or thrill to her tiniest touch. His phone calls, which you once awaited with fervor, become a familiar ring. Face it, we get used to things. Even the best experiences, when repeated, become ho-hum.

The Two-Year Itch

Time continues to march on. You've been together for two years now. You're still happy together and think the other is terrific. But where's the sizzle? Where's the spice?

Studies say the fizzle-on-the-sizzle effect inevitably takes place between eighteen months to two years of constant togetherness.[4] His touch no longer ignites Sparks. Her body no longer incites animal hunger. But here's the real tragedy: Many couples feel that love is cooling along with the passion.

Last Fourth of July, I was part of the oohing and aahing crowd straining their necks staring up at the fabulous Macy's fireworks show. A family with three little tots stood next to me. Unfortunately,

Mommy and Daddy had only one pair of shoulders each. I hoisted one of the little boys up as high as I could. To me, his joyful squealing was far more exciting than the artistic explosions overhead. After the last incredible blast that lit up the sky as bright as midday, I put him down. "NO!" he howled. "It's not over. It can't be."

As his little arms stretched up for me to lift him again, I said, "I'm afraid it is over. But wasn't it beautiful?"

"No, it can't be over," he screamed again. "There's more. There's got to be." When I kneeled down and shook my head, tears flooded his eyes in disbelief.

Sadly, that's the way many couples feel when the fireworks in a relationship are over. When the deliciously passionate drugs of phase one diminish or disappear, they face a dilemma. They look at each other through tears and ask themselves, "Is love really over?"

"No! No! No!" I want to shout at these people who once passionately loved each other. Robert Browning grasped the truth when he wrote, "The last of love for which the first was made. . . . The best is yet to come."[5]

And neuroscience agrees.

You may have been devastated when you discovered the Tooth Fairy and Santa Claus were myths. But because of what you're going to learn in the rest of this chapter, you don't need to fear that "happily ever after" will be next.

A Little Mouse in the Meadow Holds a Secret of Togetherness

If you've been buried in neuroscience night and day for the past few years as I have, you're probably sick to death of hearing about the prairie vole. I was too—at first. Until I fell in love with the little creature. Everyone does, except farmers whose crops he chomps on. When you hear more about this cute critter's lifestyle, you'll love him too.

Many people mistake this tiny animal that lives in the prairies and meadows for a mouse, but he's got stockier legs, a shorter tail, teensy eyes, and almost hidden ears. He is absolutely adorable and very admirable.

The loveliest thing about these little meadow mice is that when they fall in love and mate, they stay together forever.[6] Upon meeting his future lifelong partner, the male has wild round-the-clock love-making with her for twenty-four hours. After that he's a goner. The couple sleeps cuddled together, grooms each other, and raises the kids together as loving parents.

Unlike the nasty lab rat we discussed earlier, this faithful little meadow mouse won't even look at another female. The experiment proving this is amazing to watch. Researchers put the "husband" meadow mouse in a center cage sandwiched between two other cages.[7] One adjoining cage contains his "wife" and on the opposite side "the other woman." No matter how hot the other female may be—for a meadow mouse, that is—he won't even go sniff her out. He prefers the side of the cage closest to his "wife."

Infidelity is practically unheard of in his species. If his true love dies, it's a rare meadow mouse that will go on to "marry" again.[8] The big question: Why is this faithful mouse so different from practically all other male mammals, birds, and fish in our world?

You may have guessed. It's Chemistry, of course. Just like humans falling in love and staying in love, his devotion comes from naturally produced substances. The first time the two furry little creatures have sex, a big dose of the bonding chemicals we've discussed, oxytocin and vasopressin, flood through their systems. In the prairie vole it sticks. And here's what's so amazing. Without these chemicals they would become sexually promiscuous rats.[9] In fact, when lab scientists extracted the fidelity chemicals from the devoted little male, he started chasing tail just as much as other species. In addition, his true love's motherly instinct went right out the cage window.

There is another 99 percent genetically identical animal called the "montane vole." (I'll give Cognitive Science students time to hiss.) He is a real bastard when it comes to family values. After having sex Pop runs off immediately to find a hotter new mouse. And it's not just Dad who drops the family. Mom also abandons her babies soon after birth.[10] At least the kids don't have any deep psychological problems with it. They just shrug it off, grow up, and repeat the whole dysfunctional process. And to think that the only difference between the loving mice and the lousy mice is a few drops of oxytocin and vasopressin!

"Oh, no," you may be thinking. "Are you trying to tell me all those beautiful heartfelt, lasting emotional bonds come down to chemicals?" I suppose one could look at it that way (neuroscience does), but here's another. Like all emotions, sentiments of love, devotion, and commitment emanate from your brain. When your brain feels those sentiments, it manufactures chemicals—chemicals that create and influence feelings. So it's the story of which came first, the chicken or the egg? Or in this case, the chemicals or the emotions? And does it really matter?

The good news is that there are methods to create the loving chemicals in your lasting Love Partner's brain. You don't need to drug her with pills, inhalers, or liquids. You don't need to slip secret substances into his beer. There are actual techniques, Chemistry Sparkers, to make the brain and body of your Love Partner naturally produce these exquisite chemicals.

Do I sound like a hack hawking a hair-growing magic potion from a stagecoach bandstand?

I would understand if you answered "yes" to my question. It does sound preposterous, doesn't it? But brain imaging doesn't lie.

How to Spark Long-Lasting Chemistry Anywhere, Anytime

One of the easiest methods of stimulating oxytocin is speaking the primal language—touch. The human need for touch starts while enveloped in the close quarters of the womb for nine months. The fetus's more than five million skin sensory cells thrive on touch to prepare him for the large and intimidating planet he'll inhabit.

The need for human touch doesn't stop at birth. The moment you make your grand, squealing entrance into the world, you need it continually for healthy development. Something as simple as loving touch can make the difference between life and death for children in an orphanage, and its power remains throughout life until the very end.[11] Nursing homes report its phenomenal effect on residents' health, happiness, and longevity. And we now know the difference that loving touching makes on the health, happiness, and longevity of a couple.

All kinds of touch puts oxytocin in people's tanks—kissing, hugging, holding hands, an affectionate caress, even incidental toe touching the other's body while sleeping. Each touch, accidental or intended, fleeting or abiding, shoots the trust chemical into the touchee's brain and tweaks their memories for the better. Patients who were touched in casual conversation thought their doctor had stayed with them longer. Waitresses who touched got higher tips. Dentists who touched got more referrals.[12] In one study, women entering a brain scanner were told they were going to be given a shock. But when their partners touched them, their fear circuits shut down.[13]

I experienced something similar. Last year, sliding into one of those scary tubes for an MRI, I was silently freaking out. My partner, Giorgio, who was allowed to stay in the room, sensed this. He softly caressed one of my bare feet sticking out of the machine, and I relaxed like a midday snooze. Almost.

Time Out, Sports Fans

In case you think I'm getting too sentimental about touch, guys, you'll appreciate this. Teams who touch more, win more! Professors from the University of California, Berkeley filmed ninety NBA games.[14] The basketball teams who touched each other the most won the most. The Boston Celtics and the Los Angeles Lakers were the touchiest. No names here, but teams who touched the least lost the most. Even casual guy touching like high fives, fist bumps, and back slaps boost buddyship.

Gentlemen, you may think you're doing all that nonsexual touching just for her benefit. Well, your chances of getting same-night nookie are better if you affectionately touch her during the day. Don't forget, her foreplay began hours, days, and weeks before. Light touch now can mean heavy sex later.

Conversely, Huntresses, you should go overboard with touch of the sexy kind. Sitting on the couch, initiate a snuggle, massage his knee, rub his chest, plant a kiss on his cheek. Use your imagination like you used to do in your Gummi bear days.

What If I'm Ticked and Don't Feel Like Touching Right Now?

Do it anyway! Even when your long-term Love Partner (LP) is grumpy, you can boost the bonding chemicals through something called "cognitive consistency," a natural phenomenon that means your brain and body struggle to be in agreement. It's like when you're feeling lousy, you grumble. When you grumble, you feel lousy. Well, when you feel love, you touch. When you touch, you feel love. Imagine your brain and body holding this conversation.

Brain: Hey there, Body, whatcha doin'? I notice you're touching him a lot. What are you trying to tell me?

Body: Yeah, I noticed that too, Brain. I guess I'm telling you that that I love him.

Brain: Well, there certainly is a lot of physical evidence. I guess you're right. You really do love him.

Hunters, on the street, if she's miffed, take her hand. She may yank it away, but she'll warm up faster. Huntresses, if he's grouchy, slide closer to him on the couch. If he stiffens, ignore it. Your attempted snuggle has done its job.

♀♂ Chemistry Sparker #68

Find Any Excuse to Touch Your LP

Hunters, give her daily light kisses, nonsexual caresses, hugs, and cheek brushings. Huntresses, initiate hand holding, putting your head on his shoulder, and making loving moves. Light touching all night long is a veritable oxytocin factory. Let your foot rest against his leg. Leave your hand on her shoulder. And of course, the ultimate is "spooning,"' sleeping like little spoons in a drawer.

You've heard that people have to work to keep a relationship together. Snore. Somehow I just don't picture "working" at a relationship being much fun. Let's talk about playing together to stay together. That works wonders— just like enjoying the same activities sparked more Chemistry in dating.

Couples Who Play Together Stay Together

At the beginning of your love the two of you have a blast. Maybe movies, museums, and the beach. Perhaps bicycling, boating, bowling, or beachcombing. You think this high-dopamine life is pretty cool. You want it forever, so you move in together or marry.

But guess what? Real life happens! You no longer anxiously await the next moments when you do fun things together. He's there all the time. You're no longer wooing her, so the great dates diminish. No more picnics or discos. No more fancy restaurants or renting rowboats. Life is not as exciting, therefore you feel your Love Partner isn't.

This is due to the transference effect we talked about in Chapter 6. You're no longer connecting the concept of fun to your LP. Huntresses, you now subconsciously associate him with boring evenings in front of the TV, the computer, or the latest techno gizmo. Hunters, perhaps you feel neglected because she spends all her time with the kids.

Why did all the bicycling, boating, bowling, skateboarding, and snorkeling end? Many answer, "There's not enough time, and besides, it's too expensive." Well, you made time when you were dating. And little do couples know how much more it's going to cost them in the future by not continuing to enjoy these things after they're married. You'll spend a lot more on divorce or marriage counseling later than you will for babysitters and movie tickets now.

You needn't be concerned about the relationship just because the sex doesn't give you the roller coaster thrills it once did. That's Mother Nature's plan. But having good shared experiences can keep you on a longer-lasting fun merry-go-round. The more you do, the more dopamine speeds up the carousel and makes it a more exciting ride.

♀♂ Chemistry Sparker #69

Reinstate the Fun "Excitation Transfer" to Your LP

Ah, if only all big problems could have such a simple solution. Think of all the cool things you used to do, and make a mutual bucket list. Now go out and enjoy those thrilling activities together to raise both your dopamine levels.[15] You'll subconsciously connect the excitement to being with her. You'll think he's the reason you're having such a good time.

Laughing Is Just Another Way to Say "I Love You"

You have probably heard about the Asian laughing clubs, the endorphin-exploding health benefits of laughter, and how kids laugh six times more than adults do. I'll spare you repetition. Nor will I quote one of the unfunniest books I've ever read, Freud's *Joke and Its Relation to the Unconscious,* which tells you how laughter reinvokes the joys of childhood. I'll just give you the bottom line: Laughter is very good stuff indeed.

People—primarily of the male gender—have asked me, "But what if I'm not funny?" It doesn't matter. You may think laughter is inextricably connected to humor. Not at all! It has more to do with social interaction than it does with anything funny.[16] Those serious humor researchers I mentioned earlier recorded friends hooting, hollering, and having a great time together. They found that the majority of laughter had no relation whatsoever to anything funny. It erupted simply from the joy of being together.[17] Laughing with—not at—each other expresses joy at being with your lasting Love Partner.

Let me bring cognitive consistency and the transference effect back for a quick encore: When your body is laughing, your brain thinks you're happy and, of course, your mate thinks you're the reason for the joy.

Brain: Hey, Body, why are you laughing so much? You must be happy.

Body: Yeah, I noticed all that chuckling and stuff. I guess I am happy when I'm with my partner.

Chemistry Sparker #70

Laugh with Your Long-Term Love Partner

Laughter is contagious, a socially transmitted condition. When you laugh, your Love Partner laughs. When your Love Partner laughs, you laugh. It doesn't make any difference who started it or what it's about. Whoever is around at the time gets the credit. Find excuses to laugh, giggle, guffaw, and crack up together. It's like spraying both of you with a refreshing mist of dopamine and oxytocin.

What About Long-Term Sizzling Sex?

This is the question that always comes up. Millions of writers who are more interested in telling readers what they want to hear than revealing the truth say that you can keep the *same* early kind of intense passion alive for decades. Many of them, both best-sellers and flops, promise to keep you humping until the day you meet your maker. I put those in the fiction pile in my basement.

The media don't know, repress, or conveniently ignore the fact that there is a chemical reason for this. A few years of sex with the same person just doesn't give the same kicks because, as we've learned, dopamine diminishes with any oft-repeated pleasurable experience.

Joyously, there will always be interludes of that early sizzling sex in a marriage. Vacations and celebrations are great for that. So are those special moments when, for a multitude of reasons, you feel a tremendous rush of love. But are there ways to poke the embers in between to get them blazing constantly again?

Yes, but I don't think you'd want some of the proven "gotta have your body" hot-sex stimulators—like constant periods of separation or frequent squabbles and then a dramatic makeup. Both are dopamine boosters, but dangerous ones.[18] One unintentional derision during the dispute could be the final blow. It could hit him too hard, hurt her too much. Your emotional amygdala could turn the delicious fun-fighting-then-making-up kind of dopamine into the detesting kind. And during one too-long separation, your Love Partner might meet a tempting someone else.

"So without separations or slugging it out for excitement, can I ever put that magnificent mind-blowing kind of sex back in our relationship?" As I said at the very beginning, you can create a more magnificent kind of passion—which is really mind-blowing because only a minority of couples attain it. The most important thing to remember is: *Don't think just because sex is not as hot as it was at first that love is cooling.* It could be just the opposite!

"How could that be?" you ask. Life is unfair sometimes. Oxytocin and vasopressin, the attachment chemicals that the brain produces as love grows, actually reduce a man's testosterone.[19] Here's another of Big Mama's chemical tricks: She further diminishes it when his wife is pregnant.[20] "Why waste all that precious sperm in her when he's already got her knocked up?" she asks. During pregnancy a wife often fears that her husband no longer finds her attractive because he doesn't want sex as much. She's wrong. She's just as beautiful as ever to him. It has little to do with the big tummy and a lot to do with his lower testosterone.

There are other reasons long-term sex doesn't give the same fireworks. Your caudate nucleus, or reward center, which has that nasty habit of living in the future, isn't looking forward to anything new with the same partner.[21] A Hunter knows how his wife looks when she's hot. A Huntress knows how her husband sounds when he comes. No sexual surprises are around the corner, so the lights on *Pleasure Island* dim a little.[22]

Then there is the simple aging process. Mother Nature doesn't give a flying toot about human humping later in the game. Because she's so obsessed with propagation, she has no vested interest in you staying together much beyond childbearing. In her opinion, "Why even have sex after menopause?"

Okay, so that's the bad news.

Here's the Good News—No, the Great News!

With devotion, respect, support, and emotional intimacy, a different type of powerful desire for each other grows.[23] Sure, he no longer ravishes her like a rabbit on Viagra, and her screams don't disturb the neighbors every night. But sex is more fulfilling because this time it grows out of deep oxytocin-filled love, not a raging testosterone rush. Your hot sex can develop into warm long-term lovemaking by using some of the other concoctions in MN's chemistry set—the same ones she injects into new parents to bond them to the amazing baby they created together.[24] By using the touch, laughter, and doing things together we discussed, you create the bonding chemical that encourages continued warm lovemaking. That kind is fulfilling not only physically but also emotionally.

Throughout history, all around the world people have sought aphrodisiacs such as the highly touted Spanish Fly, the Jamaican cow cod soup, Taiwanese deer penis, Asian dried lizard, and even (yuck) sick sperm whale vomit.[25] None are as effective, however, as the following. This aphrodisiac to extend sexual desire for each other is an unspoken trade deal based on the irrefutable time honored "Give and ye shall receive" doctrine.

Hunters, you're going to love the first. Huntresses, the second is for you.

Why "Quickies" Count

Huntresses, sweet lovemaking for us means luxuriating in deep kisses, slow caresses, loving words—maybe even a foot massage if we "get lucky"—then the hot sex. But for a male, as much as he loves you, his main interest is the big finale. Unfortunately, Mother Nature is on his side, because his caressing your body does nothing for her propagation goal. His orgasm does.

Let's say you're now living together. It's a typical weeknight. You're both exhausted. The heartless alarm will blast you out of bed in six hours. But your testosterone-filled sweetie is all set to go and craves some high-speed mingling of limbs. For you to really enjoy it, however, you need some sensual stroking, licking, and loving. On average it takes eighteen minutes to bring us women to orgasm. He can do the job in eight to eighteen thrusts.[26]

Have mercy, Huntresses. It's a tall order for a tired male to slow down and start the quarter of an hour minimum process of warming you up by giving proper attention to the countless super-sensitive areas all over your body. You're tired too, and because quickies aren't as fulfilling for you, perhaps you feign a headache. Now he feels unloved.

Think about it, girl. It takes it more time for you to hem and haw about a headache than for him to be fully satisfied. Sure you might not be in the mood right now, but never forget that he interprets a quickie as your love for him.

Here's the reason quickies can literally keep the Chemistry between you alive. With repetition, the bonding oxytocin and vasopressin that flood his brain at ejaculation have a cumulative effect on his feelings of togetherness with you.[27] He associates, or in neurolinguistic programming terms, "anchors" his joy of sex with you.

An added benefit is oxytocin's talent for burying unpleasant memories.[28] If he's flaming mad at you for any reason, his ejaculation acts as a fire extinguisher.

♀ Chemistry Sparker #71

Give Him Lots of "Quickie" Bonding

Girl, look at it this way: Constant sex plays a bigger role for a male, and you wanting it with him demonstrates your love. The chemicals released in his brain accumulate over the long term. And just think: A quickie can take less than five minutes.

So you must decide if quickies are worth it. If you ask him to slow down every time, *he* just may figure it's not worth it. Compromise.

I was discussing this chapter with a friend of mine who has been married for eight years, and whenever I see her with her husband, it's obvious that he's still deeply in love with her. In one of those girl-talk moments, she said quickies are part of their regular love life. She would never tell her husband, but she jokingly said, "I think of it as 'taking one for the team.'" In fact, she initiates the quickies every so often. It's part of keeping "the team" together.

Incidentally, don't feel you need to compete with Meg Ryan's infamous fake deli orgasm in the movie *When Harry Met Sally*. In fact, don't fake it during a quickie because he may think his speedy style is all you want. Tell him you enjoy it too because you love him. But do tell him how you love it even more when it's long and slow. Save your "Oh, oh, yes, yes, YESSSSS!" for the incredible real ones he'll want to give you when there's more time.

Turnabout Is Fair Foreplay

Hunters, now it's time for you to "give one for the team." Whenever there's time, thrill her with the tender leisurely lovemaking she longs for—and make time more often. She craves those as much as you crave quickies.

Gentlemen, to increase the sexual Chemistry between you and your Love Partner, I suggest you go back and reread the Sparkers in Chapter 7:

- Chemistry Sparker number 46: *Set the Stage for Sex*. Creating her desired erotic atmosphere is just as important now. What kind of music puts her in the mood? Does she prefer dim lighting? Does she like a back rub or a foot massage before the action begins?

- Chemistry Sparker 47: *Let Her Start the Strip.* You can start the strip now—but of *her* clothes, not yours. While tenderly unbuttoning her blouse, express how much you care for her. Kiss her shoulder as you gently slip the top of her nightgown to the side. No quickies now. This is her time. Think "Slowies." Slow and sweet.
- Chemistry Sparker 48: *Don't Get Physical, Get Oral.* Your tender words mean more to her now than ever, and you can truthfully use the "L" word. Say it often—and not just during sex.
- Chemistry Sparker 49: *Play in Her Secret Garden.* You no longer need to ask what she wants because you're already familiar with her erotic paradise. Visit it with her frequently.
- And, of course, give yourself a refresher on Sparker 50: *Geography 101 for Hunters.*

Earlier I suggested that women read magazines that show the average man's attitude toward sex. Turnabout is only fair play here too. Pick up a copy of *Cosmopolitan*. One cursory page flipping suffices to see the setting for sex through your lady's eyes. You'll find beautiful bedding, an occasional candle, and the omnipresent admiring and loving expression on the face of the male she's having sex with.

Chemistry Sparker #72

Don't Think "Sex." Think "Seduction."

Courting doesn't end at the altar, and neither do seduction techniques. Now that you know all the hidden pathways in her secret sexual garden, explore each one unhurriedly. The chemicals created during foreplay have an especially endearing and enduring effect on a Huntress.

Everyone Has Something They Need to Hear

Every decade or so, a TV commercial comes along that makes you think, "Wow, I gotta get one of those thingamajigs." This was not one of them, and I do not even recommend their product. But we can learn a lot from their advertising campaign.

Madison Avenue types spend millions of dollars annually for focus groups to discover what consumers want to hear and then pay millions more for just the right actors to dramatize it. This particular commercial is on target and gives great insight into the sentiments that your long-term Love Partner hungers to hear from you.

The following individuals flashed on screen for three seconds and delivered one line each into the camera. Here are the numbered characters, and their one-liners are in the alphabetized list below it. Figure out what each person wanted to hear and fill in the letter next to the desired expressions.

1) Frazzled woman in a suburban home, dishes piled in the background, trying to control her frisky infant
2) Rushed thirtyish middle-management male straightening his tie getting ready for work
3) Kindly old man sitting alone on a park bench
4) Young woman looking into the camera flirtatiously
5) Poignantly smiling bald woman who had lost her hair obviously due to chemotherapy
6) Male teenager making a video of his face on his computer for his girlfriend
7) Ten-year-old kid in a superman costume

Here are their one-line scripts. See if you can match the people above to what they most wanted to hear.

___ a) *"Tell me* we'll stay together forever, in sickness and in health."

___ b) *"Tell me* we'll grow old together."

___ c) *"Tell me* I'm still beautiful."

___ d) *"Tell me* you need me."

___ e) *"Tell me* you miss me."

___ f) *"Tell me* that I'm your superhero."

___ g) *"Tell me* you love me."

The Answers: a) 5; b) 3; c) 1; d) 2; e) 6; f) 7; g) 4

⚥ Chemistry Sparker #73

Say What Your Long-Term Love Partner Needs to Hear

Grow an extra antenna to pick up precisely what your Love Partner needs from you emotionally. Then find a hundred ways to repeat this truth over and over. She will never tire of hearing it. He will feel closer to you every time you say it.

In this case, you needn't feel hesitant about making gender-stereotyped generalizations. Hunters and Huntresses need to hear different things to get long-lasting love chemicals flowing through their brains.

I'm embarrassed to reveal that it was a Hallmark Card Valentine's Day commercial. (Yes, sometimes a flower grows in dung, and this was such a blossom in a stench-filled field of TV ads.) The final line speaks the truth: "Everyone has something they need to hear."

It is often said, "Life is not a Hallmark card." That's true, but in long-lasting love it's beautiful to make it sound like one.

Hunters, *Why* Her Feeling Loved Creates Lasting Chemistry

Evolutionary psychologists once tucked all human behavior into an envelope neatly labeled "Evolution" and sealed the flap. They figured that, although we now reside in cities and suburbs rather than jungles and woods, we still needed precisely the same ancient toolbox between the ears. Then neuroscience and developmental evolution discovered that our brains are changing more quickly than expected. However, especially in the framework of love relationships, it's pretty clear that ancient influences continue to have a strong foothold in our thinking.

Chemistry Sparker #74

Give Her a Daily Dose of What She *Really* Needs

Hunters, at least once a day—minimum—tell your long-term Love Partner that you love her. And no matter what happens, bite your tongue before saying anything that she could, in the furthest stretch of her imagination, possibly interpret as "I don't love you anymore." If you do, her Cro-Magnon grandmother will tell her, "Girl, you're as good as dead."

Females know that if a man loves a woman, he stays with her. And up until recently, Mom needed a Hunter for both of them to survive. So she had a vested interest in being loved by her man for a very long time. In her mind, love equals survival. Thus, she *needs* a man's love.

A Hunter, of course, wants to be loved too. But a male doesn't need it as much because ancient voices are not echoing that he can't survive unless a woman protects him.

Once I was being interviewed as the guest expert on a show with four couples going through the two-year itch. The host asked the guys, "When was the last time you told your wife you loved her?" One responded, "I told her I loved her when I married her. If anything changes, I'll let her know." Every woman in the audience wanted to hurl rotten tomatoes at him.

Huntresses, *Why* His Feeling Needed Creates Lasting Chemistry

I decided to web search the question: "Why doesn't he tell me he loves me?" At this writing, the question got 110 million hits from women asking precisely that. Yet I didn't get one hit from a man complaining, "Why doesn't she tell me she needs me?" In fact, a search on "Why doesn't she tell me she needs me" first brought up a woman asking about her toddler, "Why doesn't she tell me she needs me . . . to take her to the potty?"

A man craves being needed by you as much as you hunger for his love. Buried deep in his brain, his brawny hirsute heroic club-carrying ancestor is alive and well. Because the womenfolk's lives depended on his wonderfulness, he got used to being dauntless and depended on.

Sisters, if you have ever dreamt about being swept up by the handsome prince, why can't he dream of being Prince Valiant? When you can't fix the electrical wire in a lamp, he wants to come riding into the living room on his white steed, shouting, "Fear not, sweet damsel! I will rescue you from this dilemma." So, ladies, let him. And bite your tongue until it's bloody before giving him advice on how to go about doing it.

♀ Chemistry Sparker #75

Find Ways to Say "I Need You"

It's not just your guy. Practically all males have a neurological need to provide the solution to problems, especially his woman's. I've read dozens of books like *1000 Ways to Say I Love You*. Nice stuff. But there aren't any on *1000 Ways to Say I Need You to Your Man*. In fact, not even *One Way to Say I Need You to Your Man*. Start noodling on some now and express them often.

"To What Do You Credit Your Lifelong Love?"

Looking out my window some winters in New York City, I expect to see polar bears strolling down my street. That's when I try to escape to Sarasota, Florida, for a mini-vacation. Even more beautiful than the sun and the sea there are the elder couples I see, some bicycling or kayaking together. Others strolling hand in hand or helping a partner in a walker navigate a grocery store aisle. I befriended several of the aging couples and learned a lot about the exquisite beauty and contentment that comes with long-term togetherness.

Recently I saw a TV talk show host interviewing half a dozen happy couples who had passed their fiftieth anniversary. Some had canes, a few were in wheelchairs, and most were holding hands. Their kisses were for the camera, but their sincere smiles were for their lifelong mates. Yes, a couple can stay in love forever.[29]

Naturally the host asked, "To what do you credit your lifelong love?"

One septuagenarian answered, "Because I didn't marry a woman I could live with. I married the woman I couldn't live without."

There was a resounding "aww" from the studio audience. Another octogenarian lady replied, "Because my husband often buys two roses, saying, 'One is for the woman I love. The other for my best friend.' He gives them both to me."

A crescendo of longer "awws" surged from the audience.

Finally a feeble old man with a wavering voice said, "From the moment I saw her at age eighteen, I knew life without her wouldn't be worth living." He then took her hand and kissed it. The audience reaction was something approaching a simultaneous group orgasm that lasted about five minutes.

If one of those octogenarians knew as much about neuroscience as you now do, his answer to the question would have been less romantic but more scientifically accurate. His frail voice would have murmured, "It's because we knew about the chemicals affecting our brains and how to create the good ones. This wisdom and nurturing the valuable chemicals has kept us happily together."

The audience reaction would have been stunned silence, thinking the poor old goat had gone off his rocker.

And yet the Chemistry they created together was one of the reasons they were still on earth to talk about their love. Long-term Love Partners live longer lives than people who reside alone.[30] Oxytocin and vasopressin gently swim through the rivers in your brain during long-term love, making you astronomically healthier. It's not like early stage love, when dopamine and serotonin levels spike up and down like an electroencephalogram of a grasshopper in a frying pan. The attachment chemicals you create don't have the terrifying "Side effects may include" warning that TV ads spit out at the speed of light about hyperactivity, loss of appetite, compulsive acts, and symptoms associated with mental illness.[31] There is no need to "Ask your doctor if long-term togetherness is right for you." It has been proven that it is.

What to Expect When You're Expecting Lasting Love

During the early crazy-in-love, passionate, gotta-have-you-round-the-clock days and nights, the sizzling chemicals swirl. Dopamine shoots through your brains like meteors. When he caresses your cheek, dopamine and estrogen party. When she brushes against your body, dopamine and testosterone do a dizzying dance. Serotonin swims through the synapses, and your caudate nucleus flashes like a neon sign.

After a few years of living together dopamine levels dip, but there are magnificent spikes, especially when you do thrilling things with each other and laugh together. When you make love, a myriad of both the hot and the bonding chemicals intermingle. Sometimes sex is fast when time is tight. Sometimes lingering and loving, like on weekends and vacations.

When kids come, an avalanche of chemicals consumes you. Testosterone and estrogen rise and fall like a roller coaster. Huntresses, you swim in an ocean of oxytocin while bonding with your baby. Hunters, big waves of vasopressin overcome you, especially when holding your

newborn infant. There are problems, of course, and the frenetic fluc-
tuating chemicals can cause frenzy and doubt. That is the time to cling
together and not make foolish mistakes just because Mother Nature
is making you antsy to move on.

When you have similar beliefs and definitions of togetherness,
when you enjoy doing things together, when you can depend on the
other in adversity and help each other reach life goals, a fortress of
oxytocin and vasopressin approaches like a gentle mist and engulfs
you in contentment.

As you grow even older, naturally estrogen and testosterone levels
go down, but without gushing testosterone fighting the bonding
chemicals, you become closer, and Dad becomes a stronger bonder.
That's when you reach the state Bernières spoke of when he wrote
that "your roots have become so entwined together that it is inconceivable that you should ever part."

I wish you the lasting love you so richly deserve.

Stay in touch! The only thing I *don't* like about being a writer is not having the pleasure of meeting my readers. I'd love to hear from you, and you can contact me through my website, www.greatcommunicating.com. Ask a question or just let me know your thoughts.

While you're visiting the site, sign up for my free, very short monthly hint to make you an even better communicator in your professional life, your social life, and your love life.

References

Prologue

1. Robert Sapolsky, *Biology and Human Behavior: The Neurological Origins of Individuality*, 2nd ed. (Chantilly, VA: The Teaching Company, 2005).

2. John Money, *Lovemaps: Clinical Concepts of Sexual/Erotic Health and Pathology, Paraphilia, and Gender Transposition of Childhood, Adolescence, and Maturity* (New York: Irvington, 1986).

3. D. J. Siegel, *The Developing Mind: Toward a Neurobiology of Interpersonal Experience* (New York: Guilford, 1999).

4. Money, *Lovemaps*.

5. Tamas Bereczkei, Petra Gyuris, and Glenn E. Weisfeld, "Sexual Imprinting in Human Mate Choice," *Proceedings of the Royal Society of Biological Sciences* 271, no. 1544 (2004): 1129–1134.

6. Sapolsky, *Biology and Human Behavior*.

7. Ingrid R. Olson and Christy Marshuetz, "Facial Attractiveness Is Appraised in a Glance," *Emotion* 5, no. 4 (December 2005): 498–502.

8. Steven W. Gangestad, Christine E. Garver-Apgar, Jeffry A. Simpson, and Alita J. Cousins, "Changes in Women's Mate Preferences Across the Ovulatory Cycle," *Journal of Personality and Social Psychology* 92, no. 1 (January 2007): 151–163.

9. Andreas Bartels and Semir Zeki, "The Neural Basis of Romantic Love," *NeuroReport* 2, no. 17 (2000): 12–15.

10. Helen Fisher, *Why We Love: The Nature and Chemistry of Romantic Love* (New York: Henry Holt and Company, 2004).

11. Arthur Aron, Helen Fisher, Debra J. Mashek, Greg Strong, and Haifang Li, and Lucy L. Brown, "Reward, Motivation, and Emotion Systems Associated with Early Stage Romantic Love," *Journal of Neurophysiology* 94, no. 1 (July 2005): 327–337.

12. Paula Tucker and Arthur Aron, "Passionate Love and Marital Satisfaction at Key Transition Points in the Family Life Cycle," *Journal of Social and Clinical Psychology* 12, no. 2 (1993): 135–147.

13. Aldous Huxley, *The Doors of Perception* (London: Chatto and Windus, 1954).

14. Zeenat F. Zaidi, "Gender Differences in Human Brain: A Review," *The Open Anatomy Journal* 2, no. 1 (2010): 37–55.

15. Pierce J. Howard, *The Owner's Manual for the Brain: Everyday Applications from Mind-Brain Research,* 3rd ed. (Austin, TX: Bard Press, 2006).

16. Douglas T. Kenrick, Edward K. Sadalla, Gary Groth, and Melanie R. Trost, "Evolution, Traits, and the Stages of Human Courtship," *Journal of Personality* 58, no. 1 (March 1990), 97–116.

17. Steven W. Gangestad and Jeffry A. Simpson, "The Evolution of Human Mating: Trade-Offs and Strategic Pluralism," *Behavioral and Brain Sciences,* 23, no. 4 (2000) 573–587.

18. Bianca P. Acevedo, Arthur Aron, Helen E. Fisher, and L. L. Brown, "Neural Correlates of Long-Term Intense Romantic Love," *Social Cognitive and Affective Neuroscience* 7, no. 2 (February 2012): 145–159.

19. Fisher, *Why We Love.*

20. Sapolsky, *Biology and Human Behavior.*

21. Jeffry A. Simpson and Steven W. Gangestad, "Individual Differences in Sociosexuality: Evidence for Convergent and Discriminant Validity," *Journal of Personality and Social Psychology* 60, no. 6 (June 1991): 870–883.

22. William G. Axinn and Arland Thornton, "The Transformation in the Meaning of Marriage," in *The Ties That Bind: Perspectives on Marriage and Cohabitation,* edited by Linda J. Waite, 147–165 (New York: De Gruyter,

2000); Susan Sprecher, Amy Wenzel, and John H. Harvey, eds., *Handbook of Relationship Initiation* (New York: Psychology Press, 2008).

23. Alan S.Gurman, ed., *Clinical Handbook of Couple Therapy*, 4th ed. (New York: Guilford Press, 2008).

Chapter 1

1. Pierce J. Howard, *The Owner's Manual for the Brain: Everyday Applications for Mind-Brain Research,* 3rd ed. (Austin, TX: Bard Press, 2006).

2. Robert J. Sternberg and Susan Grajek, "The Nature of Love," *Journal of Personality and Social Psychology* 47, no. (3) (1984): 12–29.

3. Anne Moir and David Jessel, *Brain Sex: The Real Difference Between Men and Women* (New York: Dell, 1991).

4. Ibid.

5. Ibid.

6. Howard, *The Owner's Manual for the Brain.*

7. Robert Sapolsky, *Biology and Human Behavior: The Neurological Origins of Individuality,* 2nd ed. (Chantilly, VA: The Teaching Company, 2005).

8. Sandra L. Murray and John G. Holmes, "A Leap of Faith? Positive Illusions in Romantic Relationships," *Personality and Social Psychology Bulletin* 23, no. 6 (1997): 586–604.

9. Helen Fisher, *Why We Love: The Nature and Chemistry of Romantic Love* (New York: Henry Holt and Company, 2004).

10. Helen Fisher and J. Anderson Thomson Jr., "Lust, Romance, Attraction, Attachment: Do The Side-Effects Of Serotonin-Enhancing Antidepressants Jeopardize Romantic Love, Marriage and Fertility?" in *Evolutionary Cognitive Neuroscience,* edited by Steven M. Platek, Julian Paul Kennan, and Todd K. Shakleford, 245–283 (Cambridge, MA: MIT Press, 2007).

11. Malcolm Caruthers, *The Testosterone Revolution: Rediscover Your Energy and Overcome the Symptoms of Male Menopause* (London: Thorsons, 2001).

12. Thomas R. Insel, "Oxytocin—A Neuropeptide for Affiliation: Evidence from Behavioral, Receptor Autoradiographic, and Comparative Studies," *Psychoneuroendocrinology* 17, no. 1 (1992): 3–35.

13. Ilanit Gordon, Orna Zagoory-Sharon, James F. Leckman, and Ruth Feldman, "Prolactin, Oxytocin, and the Development of Paternal Behavior Across the First Six Months of Fatherhood," *Hormones and Behavior* 58, no. 3 (August 2010): 513–518.

14. Lee T. Gettler, Thomas W. McWade, C. W. Kuzawa, and A.B. Feranil, "Longitudinal Evidence That Fatherhood Decreases Testosterone in Human Males," edited by A. E. Storey, Proceedings of the National Academy of Sciences of the United States of America, 108, no. 39 (September 27, 2011): 16194–16199, http://www.pnas.org/content/early/2011/09/02/1105403108 .full.pdf+html.

15. Sandra J. Berg and Katherine E. Wynne-Edwards, "Changes in Testosterone, Cortisol, and Estradiol Levels in Men Becoming Fathers," *Mayo Clinic Proceedings* 76, no. 6 (2001): 582–592.

Chapter 2

1. A. H. Veenema, and I. D. Neuman, "Central Vasopressin and Oxytocin Release: Regulation of Complex Social Behaviors," *Progress in Brain Research* 170 (2008): 261–276.

2. C. L., Clark, P. R. Shaver, and M. F. Abrahams, "Strategic Behaviors in Romantic Relationship Initiation," *Personality and Social Psychology Bulletin* 25, no. 6 (1999): 709–722.

3. William G. Axinn and Arland Thornton, "The Transformation in the Meaning of Marriage" in *The Ties That Bind: Perspectives on Marriage and Cohabitation,* edited by Linda J. Waite, 147–165 (New York: Aldine de Gruter, 2000).

4. Susan Sprecher, Amy Wenzel, and John H. Harvey, eds., *Handbook of Relationship Initiation* (New York: Psychology Press, 2008).

5. Zeenat F. Zaidi, "Gender Differences in Human Brain: A Review," *The Open Anatomy Journal* 2, no. 1 (2010): 37–55.

6. Louann Brizendine, *The Male Brain* (New York: Broadway Books, 2010).

7. Samuel Vaknin, *Malignant Self-Love: Narcissism Revisited.* (Prague: Narcissus, 2007).

8. Russell D. Clark and Elaine Hatfield, "Gender Differences in Receptivity to Sexual Offers," *Journal of Psychology and Human Sexuality* 2 (1989): 39–55.

9. Russell D. Clark, "The Impact of AIDS on Gender Differences in Willingness to Engage in Casual Sex," *Journal of Applied Social Psychology* 20, no. 9 (May 1990): 771–782.

10. Charles W. Hobart, "The Incidence of Romanticism During Courtship," *Social Forces* 36, no 4 (1958): 362–367, 364.

11. Louann Brizendine, *The Female Brain* (New York: Broadway Books, 2006).

12. Ibid.

13. David M. Buss and Todd K. Shackelford, "Attractive Women Want It All: Good Genes, Economic Investment, Parenting Proclivities, and Emotional Commitment," *Evolutionary Psychology* 6, no. 1 (2008): 134–246.

14. B. Pawlowski and L. G. Boothroyd, D. I. Perrett, S. Kluska, "Is Female Attractiveness Related to Final Reproductive Success?" *Collegium Antropologicum* 32, no. 2 (June 2008): 457–460.

15. Ibid.

16. D. Scutt and J. T., Manning, "Symmetry and Ovulation in Women," *Human Reproduction* 11, no. 11 (1996): 2477–2480.

17. John Tierney, "The Threatening Scent of Fertile Women," *New York Times,* February 21, 2011, http://www.nytimes.com/2011/02/22/science/22 tier.html.

18. Steven W. Gangestad, Christine E. Garver-Apgar, Jeffry A. Simpson, and Alita J. Cousins, "Changes in Women's Mate Preferences Across the Ovulatory Cycle," *Journal of Personality and Social Psychology* 92, no. 1 (January 2007): 151–163.

19. P. Sorokowski, "Do Men Prefer Blondes? The Influence of Hair Color on the Perception of Age and Attractiveness of Women," *Studia Psychologiczne* 44, no. 3. (2006): 77–78.

20. L. Van der Berghe and P. Frost, "Skin Color Preference, Sexual Dimorphism and Sexual Selection: A Case of Gene Co-Evolution," *Ethnic and Racial Studies* 9 (1986): 87–113.

21. Verlin Hinsz, David Matz, and Rebecca Patience, "Does Women's Hair Signal Reproductive Potential?" *Journal of Experimental Social Psychology* 37, no. e (2001): 166–172.

22. Grazyna Jasienska, Anna Ziomkiewicz, Peter T. Ellison, Susan F. Lipson, and Inger Thune, "Large Breasts and Narrow Waists Indicate High Reproductive Potential in Women," *Proceedings of the Royal Society of Biological Sciences* 271, no. 1545 (2004) 1213–1217; Pierce J. Howard, *The Owner's Manual for the Brain: Everyday Applications from Mind-Brain Research,* 3rd ed. (Austin, TX: Bard Press, 2006).

23. Bruno Laeng, Ronny Mathisen, and Jan-Are Johnsen, "Why Do Blue-Eyed Men Prefer Women with the Same Eye Color?" *Behavioral Ecology and Sociobiology* 61, no. 3 (2007): 371–384.

24. Sprecher, Wenzel, and Harvey, *Handbook of Relationship Initiation.*

25. Helen Fisher, *Why We Love: The Nature and Chemistry of Romantic Love* (New York: Henry Holt and Company, 2004).

26. Charles Darwin, *The Descent of Man, and Selection in Relation to Sex* (New York: Addison, 1871).

27. Robert Sapolsky, *Biology and Human Behavior: The Neurological Origins of Individuality,* 2nd ed. (Chantilly, VA: The Teaching Company, 2005).

28. P. M. La Cerra, "Evolved Mate Preferences in Women: Psychological Adaptations for Assessing a Man's Willingness to Invest in Offspring," (doctoral dissertation, University of California, Santa Barbara, 1994).

29. Elaine Hatfield, "What Do Women and Men Want from Love and Sex?" In *Changing Boundaries: Gender Roles and Sexual Behavior,* edited by Elizabeth R. Allgeir and Naomi B. McCormick, 106–134 (Palo Alto, CA: Mayfield, 1982).

30. David M. Buss and Michael Barnes, "Preferences in Human Mate Selection," *Journal of Personality and Social Psychology* 50 (1989): 559–570.

31. Ibid.

32. Randy Thornhill, "The Biology of Beauty," *Newsweek,* June 2, 1996, http://www.thedailybeast.com/newsweek/1996/06/02/the-biology-of-beauty.html.

33. Steven W. Gangestad, and Randy Thornhill, "Menstrual Cycle Variation in Women's Preferences for the Scent of Symmetrical Men." *Proceedings of the Royal Society of London* 265, no. 1399 (1998): 927–933.

34. Howard, *The Owner's Manual for the Brain* .

35. Ibid.

36. Ibid.

37. Ibid.

38. Ibid.

39. Ibid.

Chapter 3

1. Joan Kellerman, James Lewis, and James Laird, "Looking and Loving: The Effects of Mutual Gaze on Feelings of Romantic Love," *Journal of Research in Personality* 23, no. 2 (1989): 145–1361.

2. Mark Cook, "Gaze and Mutual Gaze in Social Encounters," *American Scientist* 65 (1977): 328–33.

3. Zick Rubin, "Measurement of Romantic Love," *Journal of Personality and Social Psychology* 16, no. 2 (1970): 265–273.

4. Timothy Perper, *Sex Signals: The Biology of Love* (Philadelphia: ISI Press, 1985).

5. Pierce J. Howard, *The Owner's Manual for the Brain: Everyday Applications from Mind-Brain Research,* 3rd ed. (Austin, TX: Bard Press, 2006).

6. William G. Iacono, "Forensic 'Lie Detection': Procedures without Scientific Basis," *Journal of Forensic Psychology Practice* 1, no. 1 (2001): 75–86.

7. E. H. Hess, "Attitude and Pupil Size" *American Scientist* 212(1965): 46–54.

8. David M. Buss and Todd K. Shackelford, "Attractive Women Want It All: Good Genes, Economic Investment, Parenting Proclivities, and Emotional Commitment," *Evolutionary Psychology* 6, no. 1 (2006): 134–146.

9. Howard, *The Owner's Manual for the Brain.*

10. Zeenat F. Zaidi, "Gender Differences in Human Brain: A Review," *The Open Anatomy Journal* 2, no. 1 (2010): 37–55.

11. Howard, *The Owner's Manual for the Brain.*

12. Timothy Perper, *Sex Signals: The Biology of Love* (Philadelphia: ISI Press, 1985).

13. Hugo D. Critchley, Christopher J. Mathias, and Raymond J. Dolan, "Neural Activity in The Human Brain Relating to Uncertainty and Arousal During Anticipation," *Neuron* 29, no. 2 (February 2001): 537–545.

14. Mark Cook and Robert McHenry, *Sexual Attraction* (New York: Pergamon Press, 1978).

15. D. P. Schmidt, and D. M. Buss, "Human Mate Poaching: Tactics and Temptations for Infiltrating Existing Mateships," *Personality and Social Psychology* 80, no. 6 (June 2001): 894–917.

16. Eric R. Bressler and Sigal Balshine, "The Influence of Humor on Desirability," *Evolution and Human Behavior* 27, no. 1 (2006): 29–39.

17. Schmidt and Buss, "Human Mate Poaching."

18. Ibid.

19. P. N. Hamid, "Changes in Person Perception as a Function of Dress," *Perceptual Motor Skills* 29, no1 (1969): 191–194.

20. Meredith L. Chivers, Michael C. Seto, and Ray Blanchard, "Gender and Sexual Orientation Differences in Sexual Response to Sexual Activities Versus Gender of Actors in Sexual Films," *Journal of Personality and Social Psychology* 93, no. 6 (2007): 1108–1121.

21. J. M. Townsend and G. D. Levy, "Effect of Potential Partner's Costume and Physical Attractiveness on Sexuality and Partner Selection," *Journal of Psychology* 124, no. 4 (1990): 371–389.

22. Chivers, Seto, and Blanchard, "Gender and Sexual Orientation Differences in Sexual Response to Sexual Activities Versus Gender of Actors in Sexual Films."

23. Howard, *The Owner's Manual for the Brain*.

24. Susan Sprecher, Amy Wenzel, and John H. Harvey, eds., *Handbook of Relationship Initiation* (New York: Psychology Press, 2008).

25. Todd K. Shackelford, David Schmitt, and David Buss, "Universal Dimensions Of Human Mate Preferences," *Personality and Individual Differences* 39 (2005): 447–458.

26. John M. Townsend and Gary D. Levy, "Effects of Potential Partner's Physical Attractiveness and Socioeconomic Status on Sexuality and Partner Selection," *Archives of Sexual Behavior* 19, no. 2 (1990): 149–164.

27. Howard, *The Owner's Manual for the Brain: Everyday Applications from Mind-Brain Research*, 3rd ed. (Austin, TX: Bard Press 2006).

28. R. K. Winkelmann, "The Erogenous Zones: Their Nerve Supply and Its Significance," *Mayo Clinic Proceedings* 34, no. 2 (1959): 39–47.

29. R. Ecochard and A. Gougeon "Side of Ovulation and Cycle Characteristics in Normally Fertile Women," *Human Reproduction* 15, no. 4 (2000): 752–755.

30. Karl Grammer, LeeAnn Renninger, and Bettina Fischer, "Disco Clothing, Female Sexual Motivation, and Relationship Status: Is She Dressed to Impress?" *Journal of Sex Research* 41, no. 1 (2004): 66–74; Meghan Provost, Vernon Quinsey, and Nikolaus Troje, "Differences in Gait Across the Menstrual Cycle and Their Attractiveness to Men," *Archives of Sexual Behavior* 37, no. 4 (2008): 598–604.

31. M. M. Moore, "Nonverbal Courtship Patterns in Women: Context and Consequences," *Ethnology and Sociobiology* 6 (1985): 237–247.

Chapter 4

1. James R. Roney, Katherine N. Hanson, Kristina M. Durante, and Dario Maestripieri, "Reading Men's Faces: Women's Mate Attractiveness Judgments Track Men's Testosterone and Interest in Infants," *Proceedings of the Royal Society of Biological Sciences* 273, no. 1598 (September 2006): 2169–2175.

2. Julie K. Hasart, Kevin L. Hutchinson, "The Effects of Eyeglasses on Perceptions of Interpersonal Attraction," *Journal of Social Behavior and Personality* 8, no. 3 (1993): 521–528.

3. Günter J. Hitsch, Ali Hortaçsu, and Dan Ariely, "What Makes You Click? Mate Preferences and Mating Outcomes in Online Dating," University of Chicago (January 2010), http://home.uchicago.edu/~ghitsch/Hitsch-Research /Guenter_Hitsch_files/Mate-Preferences.pdf.

4. A. H. Maslow, and N. L. Mintz, "Effects of Aesthetic Surroundings," *Journal of Psychology* 41 (1956): 247–254.

5. Harold Sigall and David Landy, "Radiating Beauty: The Effects of Having a Physically Attractive Partner on Person Perception," *Journal of Personality and Social Psychology* 28, no. 2 (1973): 218–224.

6. Hitsch, Hortaçsu, and Ariely, "What Makes You Click?"

7. Andrew J. Elliot and Daniela Niesta, "Romantic Red: Red Enhances Men's Attraction to Women," *Journal of Personality and Social Psychology* 95 (2008): 1150–1164.

8. Douglas T. Kendrick and Sara E. Gutierres, "Contrast Effects and Judgments of Physical Attractiveness: When Beauty Becomes a Social Problem," *Journal of Personality and Social Psychology* 38, no. 1 (1980): 131–140.

9. S. Gary Garwood, Lewis Cox, Valerie Kaplan, Neal Wasserman, and Jefferson L. Sulzer, "Beauty Is Only 'Name' Deep: The Effect of First-Name on Rating Physical Attraction," *Journal of Applied Social Psychology* 10, no. 5 (1980): 431–435.

10. Amy Perfors, "What's in a Name? The Effect of Sounds Symbolism on Perception of Facial Attractiveness," *Journal of Applied Social Psychology* 10, no. 5 (1980): 431–435.

11. John A. Bargh, Katelyn Y. A. McKenna, and Grainne M. Fitzsimons, "Can You See the Real Me? Activation and Expression of the 'True Self' on the Internet." *Journal of Social Issues* 58, no. 1 (2002): 34–80.

12. Edmond Rostad, *Cyrano de Bergerac*, Act 3.

Chapter 5

1. N. B. McCormick, T. Perper, and A. J. Jones, "Bar Hopping as Science: Results and Methodological Issues Related to Naturalistic Observational Research in Bars," Paper presented at the Eastern Region Conference of the Society for the Scientific Study of Sex, Philadelphia, April 1983.

2. Chris L. Kleinke, Frederick B. Meeker, and Richard A. Staneski, "Preference for Opening Lines: Comparing Ratings by Men and Women," *Sex Roles* 15, no. 11–12 (1986): 585–600.

3. C. L. Apicella, D. R. Feinbert, and F. W. Marlowe, "Voice Pitch Predicts Reproductive Success in Male Hunter-Gatherers," *Biology Letters* 3, no. 6 (2007): 682–684.

4. Jacquie D. Vorauer, Jessica J. Cameron, John G. Holmes, and Deanna G. Pearce, "Invisible Overtures: Fears of Rejection and the Signal Amplification Bias," *Journal of Personality and Social Psychology* 84, no. 4 (April 2003): 793–812.

5. Timothy Perper, *Sex Signals: The Biology of Love* (Philadelphia: ISI Press, 1985).

6. Debra G. Walsh and Jay Hewitt, "Giving Men the Come-On: Effect of Eye Contact and Smiling in a Bar Environment," *Perceptual and Motor Skills* 61, no. 3, pt. 1 (1985): 873–874.

7. Michael R. Cunningham, "Reactions to Heterosexual Opening Gambits: Female Selectiveness and Male Responsiveness," *Personality and Social Psychology Bulletin* 15, no.1 (March 1989): 27–41.

8. Susan Young, "Brain Chip Helps Quadriplegics Move Robotic Arms with Their Thoughts," *Technology Review*, May 16, 2002, http://www.technologyreview.com/news/427939/brain-chip-helps-quadriplegics-move-robotic-arms/.

9. Morgan Worthy, Albert L. Gary, and Gay M. Kahn, "Self-Disclosure as an Exchange Process," *Journal of Personality and Social Psychology* 13, no. 1 (1969): 59–63.

10. Jean-Phillippe Laurenceau, Lisa Feldman Barrett, and Paula R. Pietromonaco, "Intimacy as an Interpersonal Process. The Importance of Self Disclosure, Partner Disclosure, and Perceived Partner Responsiveness in Interpersonal Exchanges," *Journal of Personality and Social Psychology* 74, no. 5 (1989): 1239–1251.

11. Conor Dougherty, "Young Women's Pay Exceeds Male Peers," *Wall Street Journal*, September 1, 2010, http://online.wsj.com/article/SB10001424052748704421104575463790770831192.html.

12. Brenda Major, Patricia I. Carrington, and Peter J. D. Carnevale, "Physical Attractiveness and Self Esteem: Attributions for Praise from an Other Sex Evaluator," *Personality and Social Psychology Bulletin* 10, no. 1 (1984): 43–50.

13. David M. Buss and Michael Barnes, "Preferences in Human Mate Selection," *Journal of Personality and Social Psychology* 50 (1989): 559–570.

14. David R. Shaffer and Linda J. Pegalis, "Gender Role Orientation and Prospect of Future Interaction as Determinants of Self-Disclosure," *Personality and Social Psychology Bulletin* 22, no. 5 (May 1996): 495–506.

15. Dennis P. Carmody and Michael Lewis, "Brain Activation When Hearing One's Own and Others' Names," *Brain Research* 1116, no. 1 (October 20, 2006): 153–158.

Chapter 6

1. D. G. Dutton, and A. P. Aron, "Some Evidence for Heightened Sexual Attraction under Conditions of High Anxiety," *Journal of Personality and Social Psychology* 30, no. 4 (1974): 510–517.

2. Richard Driscoll, Keith E. Davis, and Milton E. Lipetz, "Parental Interference and Romantic Love: The Romeo and Juliet Effect," *Journal of Personality and Social Psychology* 24, no. 1 (1972): 1–10.

3. Dolf Zillmann, "Transfer of Excitation in Emotional Behavior," in *Social Psychophysiology: A Sourcebook,* edited by John T. Cacioppo and Richard E. Petty, 215–240 (New York: Guilford Press, 1983).

4. Richard Bandler and John Grinder, *Frogs into Princes: Neuro Linguistic Programming* (Moab, UT: Real People Press, 1979).

5. A. H. Maslow and N. L. Mintz, "Effects of Aesthetic Surroundings," *Journal of Psychology* 41 (1956): 247–254.

6. Shelly E. Taylor, Laura Cousino Klien, Brian P. Lewis, Tara L. Gruenewald, Regan A. R. Gurung, and John A Updegraff, "Biobehavioral Responses to Stress in Females: Tend-and-Befriend, Not Fight-or-Flight," *Psychological Review* 107, no. 3 (2000): 411–429.

7. Deborah Tannen, *You Just Don't Understand: Women and Men in Conversation* (New York: William Morrow, 1990).

8. Audrey Nelson, " The Strong Silent Type: The Male Advantage," *Psychology Today,* April 23, 2011, http://www.psychologytoday.com/blog/he-speaks-she-speaks/201104/the-strong-silent-type-the-male-advantage.

9. Azim Eiman and Dean Mobbs, Booil Jo, Vinod Menon, Allan L. Reiss, "Sex Differences in Brain Activation Elicited by Humor," *Proceedings of the National Academy of Sciences* 102, no. 45 (November 8, 2005): 16496–16501.

10. Willow Lawson, "Humor's Sexual Side," *Psychology Today,* September 1, 2005, http://www.psychologytoday.com/articles/200508/humors-sexual-side.

11. Eric R. Bressler and Sigal Balshine, "The Influence of Humor on Desirability," *Evolution and Human Behavior* 27, no. 1 (2006): 29–39.

Chapter 7

1. Daniel G. Amen, Daniel G., M.D., Sex on the Brain: 12 Lessons to Enhance Your Love Life. 2008. (New York: Crown Publishing, Harmony, 2008).

2. Ibid.

3. José L. Tlachi-López, José R. Eguibar, Alonso Fernández-Guasti, Rosa Angélica Lucio, "Copulation and Ejaculation in Male Rats Under Sexual Satiety and the Coolidge Effect," Physiology and Behavior 106, no. 5 (July 2012): 626–630.

4. Ibid.

5. Gordon Bermant and Juan M. Davidson, Biological Bases of Sexual Behavior (New York: Harper and Row, 1974).

6. Gary Stix, "Only Epilepsy Brings More Activity to Women's Brains Than Does 'Self-Stimulation' to Orgasm," Scientific American, November 15, 2011, http://blogs.scientificamerican.com/observations/2011/11/15/only-epilepsy-brings-more-activity-to-womens-brains-than-does-self-stimulation-to-orgasm/.

7. Helen Fisher, Why We Love: The Nature and Chemistry of Romantic Love (New York: Henry Holt and Company, 2004).

8. Ibid.

9. M. Kosfeld, M. Heinrichs, P. J. Zak, U. Fischbacher, and others. Fehr, "Oxytocin Increases Trust in Humans," Nature 435, no. 7042 (June 2, 2005): 673–676.

10. Ibid.

11. Pamela C. Regan and Ellen Berscheid, Love and Lust: What We Know about Human Sexual Desire (Thousand Oaks, CA: Sage Publications, 1999).

12. Deborah Blum, Sex on the Brain: The Biological Differences Between Men and Women (New York: Penguin Books, 1998).

13. Anne Moir and David Jessel, Brain Sex: The Real Difference Between Men and Women (New York: Dell Publishing, 1991)

14. Louann Brizendine, The Female Brain (New York: Broadway Books, 2006).

15. Pierce J. Howard, *The Owner's Manual for the Brain: Everyday Applications from Mind-Brain Research,* 3rd ed. (Austin, TX: Bard Press, 2006).

16. R. L. Doty, S. Applebaum, H. Zusho and R. G. Settle, "Sex Differences in Odor Identification Ability," *Neuropsychologia* 23, no. 5 (1985): 667–672.

17. G. Holstege, J. R. Georgiadis, A. M Paans, L. C. Meiners and F. H. van der Graaf, "Brain Activation During Human Male Ejaculation," *Journal of Neuroscience* 23, no. 27 (October 8, 2003): 9158–9193.

18. Meredith L. Chivers, Michael C. Seto, and Ray Blanchard, "Gender and Sexual Orientation Differences in Sexual Response to Sexual Activities Versus Gender of Actors in Sexual Films," *Journal of Personality and Social Psychology* 93, no. 6 (2007): 1108–1121.

19. B. A. Shaywitz, Sally E. Shaywitz, Kenneth R. Pugh, R. T. Constanble, and P. Skudlarski, "Sex Differences in the Functional Organization of the Brain for Language," *Nature* 373, no. 6515 (February 16, 1995): 607–609.

20. Brizendine, *The Female Brain.*

21. Roy Levin, and Cindy Meston, "Nipple/Breast Stimulation and Sexual Arousal in Young Men and Women," *Journal of Sexual Medicine* 3, no. 3 (2006): 450–454.

22. Barry R. Komisaruk and Nan Wise, "Women's Clitoris, Vagina, and Cervix Mapped on the Sensory Cortex: fMRI Evidence," *Journal of Sexual Medicine* 8, no. 10 (2011): 2822–2830.

23. A. Kilchevsky, Y. Vardi, L. Lowenstein, and I. Gruenwald, "Is the Female G-Spot Truly a Distinct Anatomic Entity?" *Journal of Sex Medicine* 9, no. 3 (2012): 719–726.

24. "30 Things To Do With a Naked Man," *Cosmopolitan,* http://www.cosmopolitan.com/sex-love/tips-moves/how-to-turn-him-on?click=main_sr#slide-1.

25. Bruce J. Ellis and Donald Symons, "Sex Differences in Sexual Fantasy: An Evolutionary Psychological Approach," *The Journal of Sex Research* 27, no. 4 (1990): 527–555.

26. Harold Leitenberg and Kris Henning, "Sexual Fantasy," *Psychological Bulletin* 117, no. 3 (May 1995): 469–496.

27. Ibid.

28. Ellis and Symons, "Sex Differences in Sexual Fantasy."

29. Brizendine, *The Female Brain*.

30. V. Apanius, D. Penn, P. R. Slev, L. R. Ruff, and W. K. Potts, "The Nature of Selection on the Major Histocompatibility Complex," *Critical Reviews in Immunology* 17, no. 2 (1997): 179–224.

31. M. Milinski, "The Major Histocompatibility Complex: Sexual Selection and Mate Choice," *Annual Review of Ecology, Evolution, and Systematics* 37 (2006): 159–186.

32. Claus Wedekind, Thomas Seebeck, Florence Bettens, and Alexander J. Paepke, "MHC-Dependent Mate Preferences in Humans," *Proceedings of the Royal Society of London: Biological Sciences* 260, no. 1359 (June 22, 1995): 245–249.

33. Helen E. Fisher, "The Biology of Attraction," *Psychology Today*, April 1, 1993, http://www.psychologytoday.com/articles/199303/the-biology-attraction.

34. "Bizarre Animal Mating Rituals," Virgin Media, http://www.virginmedia.com/digital/features/bizarre-animal-mating-rituals.php?ssid=9.

35. John Tierney, "The Threatening Scent of Fertile Women," *New York Times*, February 21, 2011, http://www.nytimes.com/2011/02/22/science/22tier.html.

36. G. Miller, J. M. Tybur, B. D. Jordan, "Ovulatory Cycle Effects on Tip Earnings by Lap Dancers: Economic Evidence for Human Estrus?" *Evolution and Human Behavior* 28, no. 6 (2007): 375–381.

37. S. C. Roberts, L. M. Gosling, V. Carter, and M. Petrie, "MHC-Correlated Odor Preferences in Humans and the Use of Oral Contraceptives," *Proceedings of the Royal Society of Biological Sciences* 275, no. 1652 (December 7, 2008): 2715–2722.

Chapter 8

1. John Gray, *Men Are from Mars, Women Are from Venus: A Practical Guide for Improving Communication and Getting What You Want in Your Relationships* (New York: Harper Collins, 1993).

2. Pierce J. Howard, *The Owner's Manual for the Brain: Everyday Applications from Mind-Brain Research,* 3rd ed. (Austin, TX: Bard Press, 2006).

3. Ibid.

4. Joseph Rhawn, *NeuroTheology: Brain, Science, Spirituality, Religious Experience* (San Jose, CA: University Press, 2003). Italics added.

5. Zeenat F. Zaidi, "Gender Differences in Human Brain: A Review," *The Open Anatomy Journal* 2 (2010): 37–55.

6. Deborah Tannen, *You Just Don't Understand: Women and Men in Conversation* (New York: William Morrow, 1990).

7. Zaidi, "Gender Differences in Human Brain."

8. Paul Ekman, *Emotions Revealed: Recognizing Faces and Feelings to Improve Communication and Emotional Life,* 2nd ed. (New York: Henry Holt and Co., 2007).

9. Ibid.

10. Howard, *The Owner's Manual for the Brain.*

11. Louann Brizendine, *The Male Brain* (New York: Broadway Books, 2010).

12. Howard, *The Owner's Manual for the Brain.*

Chapter 9

1. Susan S. Hendrick and Clyde Hendrick, "Gender Differences and Similarities in Sex and Love," *Personal Relationships* 2 (1995): 55–65.

2. Donn Byrne, "Interpersonal Attraction and Attitude Similarity," *Journal of Abnormal Social Psychology* 62 (May 1961): 713–715.

3. Theodore M. Newcomb, *The Acquaintance Process* (New York: Holt, Rinehart and Wilson, 1961).

4. Byrne, "Interpersonal Attraction and Attitude Similarity.

5. John Mordechai Gottman and Nan Silver, *Why Marriages Succeed or Fail* (New York: Simon and Schuster, 1994).

6. G. J. Fletcher, J. A. Simpson, G. Thomas, and L. Giles, "Ideals in Intimate Relationships," *Journal of Personality and Social Psychology* 76, no. 1 (1999): 72–89.

7. John W. Thibaut and Harold H. Kellel, *The Social Psychology of Groups* (New York: Wiley, 1959).

8. Mario Mikulincer and Gail S. Goodman, eds., *Dynamics of Romantic Love: Attachment, Caregiving, and Sex* (New York: Guilford Press, 2006).

9. A. Aron, E. N. Aron, and C. Norman, "The Self Expansion Model of Motivation and Cognition in Close Relationships and Beyond," In *Blackwell Handbook in Social Psychology, vol. 2: Interpersonal Processes*, edited by M. Clark and G. Fletcher, 478–501 (Oxford: Blackwell, 2001).

10. Tara Parker-Pope, "The Happy Marriage Is the 'Me' Marriage," *New York Times,* December 31, 2010, http://www.nytimes.com/2011/01/02/week inreview/02parkerpope.html.

11. Jay Belsky, Laurence Steinberg, and Patricia Draper, "Childhood Experience, Interpersonal Development, and Reproductive Strategy: An Evolutionary Theory of Socialization," *Child Development* 62, no. 4 (1991): 647–670.

12. Ibid.

13. Pedro M. Pereyra, Weixian Zhang, and Matthias Schmidt, and Laurence E. Becker, "Development of Myelinated and Unmyelinated Fibers of Human Vagus Nerve During the First Year of Life," *Journal of the Neurological Sciences* 110, no. 1–2 (July 1992): 107–113.

14. J. N. Giedd, "Structural Magnetic Resonance Imaging of the Adolescent Brain," *Annals of the New York Academy of Sciences* 1021 (June 2004): 77–85.

15. H. E. Fisher, A. Aron, D. Mashek, H. Li, and L. L. Brown, "Defining the Brain Systems of Lust, Romantic Attraction, and Attachment," *Archives of Sexual Behavior* 31, no. 5 (2002): 413–419. Italics added.

Chapter 10

1. "The Fair Youth of the Shakespeare Sonnets," The Monument: Shakespeare's Sonnets, http://www.shakespearesmonument.com/page10.html.

2. Louis de Bernières, *Corelli's Mandolin* (New York: Vintage Books, 1994).

3. Sadie Leder, "From Bride to Blues: Examining the Prevalence of Post-Nuptial Depression," Science of Relationships, http://www.scienceof

relationships.com/home/2012/7/16/from-bride-to-blues-examining-the -prevalence-of-post-nuptial.html.

4. D. Marazziti and D. Canale, "Hormonal Changes When Falling in Love," *Psychoneuroendocrinology* 29, no. 7 (August 2004): 931–936.

5. Robert Browning, "Grow Old Along with Me."

6. Thomas T. Insel and C. Sue Carter, "The Monogamous Brain," *Natural History* 104, no. 8 (1995): 12–14; Mary M. Cho, A. Courtney DeVries, Jessie R. Williams, and C. Sue Carter, "The Effects of Oxytocin and Vasopressin on Partner Preferences in Male and Female Prairie Voles," *Behavioral Neuroscience* 113, no. 5 (1999): 1071–1079.

7. Ibid.

8. Ibid.

9. James T. Winslow, Nick Hastings, C. Sue Carter, Carroll R. Harbaugh, and Thomas R. Insel, "A Role for Central Vasopressin in Pair Bonding in Monogamous Prairie Voles," *Letters to Nature*, http://research.yerkes.emory .edu/Young/Getz/1993%20Winslow%20N.pdf.

10. Thomas R. Insel, and Lawrence E. Shapiroirie, "Oxytocin Receptor Distribution Reflects Social Organization in Monogamous and Polygamous Voles," *Proceedings of the National Academy of Sciences* 89, no. 13 (1992): 5981–5985.

11. Phyllis K. Davis, *The Power of Touch: The Basis for Survival, Health, Intimacy, and Emotional Well-Being* (Carlsbad, CA: Hay House, 1999).

12. Allan Pease and Barbara Pease, *The Definitive Book of Body Language* (New York: Bantam Books, 2006); James. E. Sheridan, "Marriage Advice: Touch Is a Key to a Truly Good Marriage," *News Sentinel*, October 25, 2011, http://www.news-sentinel.com/apps/pbcs.dll/article?AID=/20111025 /NEWS01/310269994.

13. Diane Ackerman, "The Brain on Love," *New York Times*, March 24, 2012, http://opinionator.blogs.nytimes.com/2012/03/24/the-brain-on-love/.

14. Michael W. Kraus, Cassy Huang, and Dacher Keltner, "Tactile Communication, Cooperation, and Performance: An Ethological Study of the NBA," http://socrates.berkeley.edu/~keltner/publications/kraus.huang.keltner .2010.pdf.

15. G. Strong and A. Aron, "The Effect of Shared Participation in Novel and Challenging Activities on Experienced Relationship Quality: Is It Mediated by High Positive Affect?" In *Self and Relationships: Connecting Intrapersonal and Interpersonal Processes,* edited by Kathleen D. Vohs and Eli J. Finkel, 342–359 (New York: Guilford Press, 2006).

16. Robert R. Provine, "Laughter," *American Scientist* 84, no. 1 (January–February 1996): 38–47.

17. Rod A. Martin, *The Psychology of Humor: An Integrative Approach* (Waltham, MA: Elsevier Academic Press, 2006).

18. Elaine Walster and Ellen Berscheid, "Adrenaline Makes the Heart Grow Fonder," *Psychology Today,* June 1971, 47–62; David M. Buss, *The Dangerous Passion: Why Jealousy Is as Necessary as Love and Sex* (New York: Free Press, 2000).

19. Lee T. Gettler, Thomas W. McDade, Alan B. Feranil and Christopher W. Kuzawa, "Longitudinal Evidence That Fatherhood Decreases Testosterone in Human Males," *Proceedings of the National Academy of Sciences of the United States of America,* http://www.pnas.org/content/early/2011/09/02/1105403108.full.pdf+html.

20. Sandra J. Berg and Katherine E. Wynne-Edwards, "Changes in Testosterone, Cortisol, and Estradiol Levels in Men Becoming Fathers," *Mayo Clinic Proceedings* 76, no. 6 (2001): 582–592.

21. Helen Fisher, *Why We Love: The Nature and Chemistry of Romantic Love* (New York: Henry Holt and Company, 2004).

22. G. S. Berns, S. M. McClure, G. Pagnoni, and P. R. Montague, "Predictability Modulates Human Brain Response to Reward," *Journal of Neuroscience* 21, no. 8 (April 2001): 2793–2798.

23. Bianca P. Acevedo and Arthur Aron, "Does a Long-Term Relationship Kill Romantic Love?" *Review of General Psychology* 13, no. 1 (2009): 59–65.

24. Wibke Blaicher, Doris Gruber, Christian Bieglmayer, Alex M. Blaicher, and Wolfgang Knogler, "The Role of Oxytocin in Relation to Female Sexual Arousal," *Gynecologic and Obstetric Investigation* 47, no. 2 (1999): 125–126.

25. "Ambergris, aka Floating Gold," squidoo, http://www.squidoo.com/ambergrease.

26. Louann Brizendine, *The Male Brain* (New York: Broadway Books, 2010).

27. Simon LeVay, *The Sexual Brain* (Cambridge, MA: MIT Press, 1994).

28. M. Kosfeld, M. Heinrichs, P. J. Zak, U. Fischbacher, and others. Fehr, "Oxytocin Increases Trust in Humans," *Nature* 435, no. 7042 (June 2, 2005): 673–676.

29. Paula Tucker and Arthur Aron, "Passionate Love and Marital Satisfaction at Key Transition Points in the Family Life Cycle," *Journal of Social and Clinical Psychology* 12, no. 2 (1993): 135–147.

30. Howard, *The Owner's Manual for the Brain*.

31. Fisher, *Why We Love*.

About the Author

Leil Lowndes is an internationally recognized communications expert who specializes in the subconscious interactions and subliminal approaches that unknowingly take place in all interpersonal communications. She conducts seminars for major corporations, associations, universities, and the public.

She is the author of ten books, including the top-selling *How to Talk to Anyone, How to Instantly Connect with Anyone, How to Make Anyone Fall in Love with You, Undercover Sex Signals, How to be a People Magnet*, and *Good-bye to Shy*.

Prior to her work in communications, Ms. Lowndes was founder and director of *The Project*, a New York City–based not-for-profit organization, which conducted personal relationship research and counseling. She is a member of the American Association of Sex Educators, Counselors, and Therapists.

Based in New York City, Ms. Lowndes has been the guest communications expert on hundreds of television and radio programs.